CONVERSATIONS AND DIALOGUES-III

By

SWAMI VIVEKANANDA

Double 9 BOOKS

CONVERSATIONS AND DIALOGUES-III

by **SWAMI VIVEKANANDA**

ISBN: 978-93-59393-63-6

Published by

DOUBLE 9 BOOKS
2/13-B, Ansari Road, Daryaganj
New Delhi - 110002
info@double9books.com
www.double9books.com
Tel. 011-40042856

ABOUT THE AUTHOR

Swami Vivekananda was born Narendranath Datta in India on January 12, 1863. He died on July 4, 1902, and was the most important student of the Indian saint Ramakrishna. He was an important part of bringing Vedanta and Yoga to the West. He is also charged with making people more aware of other religions and making Hinduism a major world religion. Vivekananda had a lot of success at the Parliament. In the years that followed, he gave hundreds of lectures across the United States, England, and Europe to spread the main ideas of Hinduism. He also started the Vedanta Society of New York and the Vedanta Society of San Francisco, which is now the Vedanta Society of Northern California. Both of these groups became the basis for Vedanta Societies in the West. Vivekananda was one of the most important philosophers and social reformers in India at the time. He was also one of the most successful and powerful Vedanta missionaries in the West.People now think of him as one of the most important people in modern India and Hinduism. Mahatma Gandhi said that after reading Vivekananda's works, he loved his country a thousand times more.

CONTENTS

I

(From the Diary of a Disciple (Shri Sharat Chandra Chakravarty, B.A.))

(Translated from Bengali)

[Place: Belur, the rented Math premises. Year: 1898.]

Swamiji was staying at the time at the rented garden-house of Nilâmbar Bâbu where the Math had been removed from Alambazar. Arrangements had been made for Shri Ramakrishna's Tithipujâ (Nativity) on a grand scale. On the morning of the auspicious day, Swamiji personally inspected the preliminaries of the worship. The inspection over, Swamiji asked the disciple, "Well, you have brought the holy threads, I hope?"

Disciple: Yes, sir, I have. Everything is ready, as you desired. But, sir, I can't make out why so many holy threads are in requisition.

Swamiji: Every Dwijâti (Brâhmins, Kshatriyas, and Vaishyas are the Dwijatis) (twice-born) has a right to investiture with the holy thread. The Vedas themselves are authority in this matter. Whoever will come here on this sacred birthday of Shri Ramakrishna I shall invest him with the holy thread. These people have fallen from their true status, and the scriptures say that after proper expiation, those fallen in the way earn the right to investiture with the holy thread. This is the great day of Shri Ramakrishna's nativity, and men will be purified by taking his name. So the assembled devotees are to be invested with the holy thread today; do you now understand?

Disciple: I have collected, Sir, quite a good number of holy threads according to your instructions, and after the worship I shall with your permission invest the Bhaktas with them.

Swamiji: To the Bhaktas who are not Brahmins, give this Mantra of Gâyatri (here Swamiji communicated to the disciple the special Gayatris for them.) By degrees all the people of the land have to be lifted to the position of Brahmins, not to speak of the Bhaktas of Shri Ramakrishna. Each Hindu, I say, is a brother of every other, and it is we who have degraded them by our outcry, "Don't touch, don't touch!" And so the whole country has been plunged to the utmost depths of meanness, cowardice, and ignorance. These men have to be uplifted; words of hope and faith have to be proclaimed to them. We have to tell them, "You are men like us, and you have all the rights that we have." Do you understand?

Disciple: Yes, sir, it should be so.

Swamiji: Now, ask those who will take the holy thread to finish their bath in the Gangâ. Than after prostration before Shri Ramakrishna, they will have their investiture.

About forty to fifty Bhaktas then duly received the Gayatri from the disciple and were invested with the holy thread. When receiving them, Swamiji's face beamed with profound delight. A little after this, Shri Girish Chandra Ghosh arrived at the Math from Calcutta.

Now arrangements for music were made at the desire of Swamiji, and Sannyasins of the Math decorated Swamiji as a Yogin.

Swamiji now chanted with the sweetest intonation to the accompaniment of the Tânpurâ, the Sanskrit hymn beginning with – कुजन्तं रामरामेति ("repeating in a low tone the name of Rama" etc.), and when the chanting came to a close, he went on repeating with exquisite charm the holy words "Râma, Râma, Shri Râma, Râma". His eyes were half-closed, and the natural sublimity of his countenance seemed to have deepened a hundred-fold. Everybody remained spelled for over half an hour.

After the chanting of Shri Rama's name, Swamiji continued to sing a song of Tulsidas on Shri Ramachandra in the same intoxicated strain of mind. Then other music followed.

After this, Swamiji suddenly took to putting of all the decorations he had on his person and began to dress Girish Babu with them. Then he declared, "Paramhansa-deva used to say our brother is the incarnation of Bhairava (Divine companion of Shiva.). There's no distinction between him and us." Girish Babu sat speechless all the time. A piece of *geruâ* cloth was also brought, and was draped in it and uttered no word of remonstrance. For he had merged his self fully today in the wishes of his brother disciples. Swamiji now said, "Well, G. C., you are to speak to us today about Thâkur (Lord). And all of you (turning all round himself) sit quiet and attentive." Even then, Girish Babu sat motionless, voiceless like marble, absolutely lost in joy. And when at last he opened his lips, he did so to say, "Ah, what can this humble self speak of our Lord of unbounded mercy! Verily in this alone I realise his mercy, that to me, this lowly creature, He has extended the privilege of sitting and mixing on the same footing with you Sannyasins, pure from your childhood, who have renounced all lust and lucre." While speaking thus, the words choked in his throat, and he could not speak anything more.

After this, some pieces of Hindu music were rendered by Swamiji. The devotees were now called to partake of refreshments. After refreshments, Swamiji came and took his seat in the parlour on the ground-floor, and all the many visitors sat round him. Accosting a house-holder friend who had his investiture with the holy thread that day, Swamiji said, "Really you all belong to the twice-born castes, only it is long since you lost your status. From this day again you become the twice-born. Repeat the Gayatri at least a hundred times daily, won't you?" The householder expressed his assent.

Meanwhile Srijut Mahendranath Gupta (Master Mahâshaya [Venerable], or "M") appeared on the scene. Swamiji cordially received him and made him take his seat. "Master Mahashaya," said Swamiji, "this is the anniversary of Shri Ramakrishna's birthday. So you shall have to relate to us something about him." Master Mahashaya bent his head down smilingly in reply.

Just then it was announced that Swami Akhandananda had come from Murshidabad with two Pântuâs which weighed one maund and a half! All of us hurried out to see these prodigious Pantuas. When they were shown to Swamiji, he said, "Take them up to the chapel for offering."

Making Swami Akhandananda the subject of his remarks, Swamiji said to the disciple, "Mark you, what a great hero he is in work! Of fear, death and the like he has no cognisance — doggedly going on doing his own work — 'work for the welfare of the many, for the happiness of the many'."

Disciple: Sir, that power must have come to him as the result of a good deal of austerities.

Swamiji: True, power comes of austerities; but again, working for the sake of others itself constitutes Tapasyâ (practice of austerity). The karma-yogins regard work itself as part of Tapasya. As on the one hand the practice of Tapasya intensifies altruistic feelings in the devotee and actuates him to unselfish work, so also the pursuit of work for the sake of others carries the worker to the last fruition of Tapasya, namely the purification of the heart, and leads him thus to the realisation of the supreme Âtman (Self).

Disciple: But, sir, how few of us can work whole-heartedly for the sake of others from the very outset! How difficult it is for such broad-mindedness to come at all as will make men sacrifice the desire for their own happiness and devote their lives for others!

Swamiji: And how many have their minds going after Tapasya? With the attraction for lust and lucre working the other way, how many long for the realisation of God? In fact, disinterested work is quite as difficult as Tapasya. So you have no right to say anything against those who go in for work in the cause of others. If you find Tapasya to be to your liking, well, go on with it. Another may find work as congenial to himself, and you have no right to make a prohibition in his case. You seem to have the settled idea in your mind that work is no Tapasya at all!

Disciple: Yes, sir, before this I used to mean quite a different thing by Tapasya.

Swamiji: As by continuing our religious practices we gradually develop a certain determined tendency for it, so by performing disinterested work over and over again, even unwillingly, we gradually find the will merging itself in it. The inclination to work for others develops in this way, do you see? Just do some such work even though unwillingly, and then see if the actual fruit of Tapasya is realised within or not. As the outcome of work for the sake of others, the angularities of the mind get smoothed down, and men are gradually prepared for sincere self-sacrifice for the good of others.

Disciple: But, sir, what is the necessity at all for doing good to others?

Swamiji: Well, it is necessary for one's own good. We become forgetful of the ego when we think of the body as dedicated to the service of others – the body with which most complacently we identify the ego. And in the long run comes the consciousness of disembodiness. The more intently you think of the well-being of others, the more oblivious of self you become. In this way, as gradually your heart gets purified by work, you will come to feel the truth that your own Self is pervading all beings and all things. Thus it is that doing good to others constitutes a way, a means of revealing one's own Self or Âtman. Know this also to be one of the spiritual practices, a discipline for God-realisation. Its aim also is Self-realisation. Exactly as that aim is attained by Jnâna (knowledge), Bhakti (devotion) and so on, also by work for the sake of others.

Disciple: But, sir, if I am to keep thinking of others day and night, when shall I contemplate on the Atman? If I rest wholly occupied with something particular and relative, how can I realise the Atman which is Absolute?

Swamiji: The highest aim of all disciplines, all spiritual paths, is the attainment of the knowledge of Atman. If you, by being devoted to the service of others and by getting your heart purified by such work, attain to the vision of all beings as the Self, what else remains to be attained in the way of Self-realisation? Would you say that Self-realisation is the state of existing as inert matter, as this wall or as this piece of wood, for instance?

Disciple: Though that is not the meaning, yet what the scriptures speak of as the withdrawal of the Self into Its real nature consists in the arresting of all mind-functions and all work.

Swamiji: Yes, this Samâdhi of which the scriptures speak is a state not at all easy to attain. When very rarely it appears in somebody, it does not last for long; so what will he keep himself occupied with? Thus it is that after realising that state described in the scriptures, the saint sees the Self in all beings and in that consciousness devotes himself to service, so that any Karma that was yet left to be worked out through the body may exhaust itself. It is this state which has been described by the authors of the Shâstras (scriptures) as Jivanmukti, "Freedom while living".

Disciple: So after all it comes about, sir, that unless this state of Jivanmukti is attained, work for the sake of others can never be pursued in the truest sense of the term.

Swamiji: Yes, that is what the Shastras say, but they also say that work or service for the good of others leads to this state of Jivanmukti. Otherwise there would be no need on the part of the Shastras to teach a separate path of religious practice, called the Karma-Yoga.

The disciple now understood the point and became silent, and Swamiji giving up the point commenced rendering in a voice of superhuman sweetness the song composed by Babu Girish Chandra Ghosh to commemorate Shri Ramakrishna's Nativity, and beginning:

"Who art Thou lying on the lap of the poor Brahmin matron."

II

(From the Diary of a Disciple (Shri Sharat Chandra Chakravarty, B.A.))

(Translated from Bengali)

[Place: The rented Math premises at Belur. Year: 1898.]

Today Swamiji is to perform a sacrifice and install Shri Ramakrishna on the site of the new Math. The disciple has been staying at the Math since the night before, with a view to witnessing the installation ceremony.

In the morning Swamiji had his bath in the Ganga and entered the worship-room. Then he made offerings to the sacred Pâdukâs (slippers) of Shri Ramakrishna and fell to meditation.

Meditation and worship over, preparations were now made for going to the new Math premises. Swamiji himself took on his right shoulder the ashes of Shri Ramakrishna's body preserved in a copper casket, and led the van. The disciple in company with other Sannyasins brought up the rear. There was the music of bells and conchs. On his way Swamiji said to the disciple, "Shri Ramakrishna said to me, 'Wherever you will take me on your shoulders, there I will go and stay, be it under a tree or in a hut.' It is therefore that I am myself carrying him on my shoulders to the new Math grounds. Know it for certain that Shri Ramakrishna will keep his seat fixed there, for the welfare of many, for a long time to come."

Disciple: When was it that he said this to you?

Swamiji: (Pointing to the Sâdhus of the Math) Didn't you hear from them? It was at the Cossipur garden.

Disciple: I see. It was on this occasion, I suppose, that the split took place between Shri Ramakrishna's Sannyâsin and householder disciples regarding the privilege of serving him?

Swamiji: Yes, but not exactly a "split" – it was only a misunderstanding, that's all. Rest assured that among those that are Shri Ramakrishna's devotees, and have *truly* obtained his grace, there is no sect or schism, there *cannot* be – be they householders or Sannyasins. As to that kind of slight misunderstanding, do you know what it was due to? Well, each devotee colours Shri Ramakrishna in the light of his own understanding and each forms his own idea of him from his peculiar standpoint. He was, as it were, a great Sun and each one of us is eyeing him, as it were, through a different kind of colored glass and coming to look upon that one Sun as parti-coloured. Of course, it is quite true that this leads to schism in course of time. But then, such schisms rarely occur in the lifetime of those who are fortunate enough to have come in direct contact with an Avatâra. The effulgence of that Personality, who takes pleasure only in the Self, dazzles their eyes and sweeps away pride, egotism, and narrow-mindedness from their minds. Consequently they find no opportunity to create sects and party factions. They are content to offer him their heart's worship, each in his own fashion.

Disciple: Sir, do the devotees of Avatara, then view him differently notwithstanding their knowing him to be God, and does this lead the succeeding generations of their followers to limit themselves within narrow bounds and form various little sects?

Swamiji: Quite so. Hence sects are bound to form in course of time. Look, for instance, how the followers of Chaitanya Deva have been divided into two or three hundred sects; and those of Jesus hold thousands of creeds. But all those sects without exception follow Chaitanya Deva or Jesus, and none else.

Disciple: Then, perhaps, Shri Ramakrishna's followers, too, will be divided in course of time into various sects?

Swamiji: Well, of course. But then this Math that we are building will harmonise all creeds, all standpoints. Just as Shri Ramakrishna held highly liberal views, this Math, too, will be a centre for propagating similar ideas. The blazing light of universal harmony that will emanate from here will flood the whole world.

While all this was going on, the party reached the Math premises. Swamiji took the casket down from his shoulder, placed it on the carpet spread on the ground, and bowed before it touching the ground with his forehead. Others too followed suit.

Then Swamiji again sat for worship. After going through Pujâ (worship), he lighted the sacrificial fire, made oblations to it, and himself cooking Pâyasa (milk-rice with sugar) with the help of his brother-disciples, offered it to Shri Ramakrishna. Probably also he initiated certain householders on the spot that day. All this ceremony being done, Swamiji cordially addressed the assembled gentlemen and said, "Pray today all of you, heart and soul, to the holy feet of Shri Ramakrishna, that the great Avatara of this cycle that he is, he may, "For the welfare of the many, and for the happiness of the many — बहुजनहिताय बहुजनसुखाय ", reside in this holy spot from this day for a great length of time, and ever continue to make it the unique centre of harmony amongst all religions." Everyone prayed like that with folded palms. Swamiji next called the disciple and said, "None of us (Sannyasins) have any longer the right to take back this casket of Shri Ramakrishna, for we have installed him here today. It behoves you, therefore, to take it on your head back (to Nilambar Babu's garden)". Seeing that the disciple hesitated to touch the casket, Swamiji said, "No fear, touch it, you have my order." The disciple gladly obeyed the injunction, lifted the casket on his head, and moved on. He went first, next came Swamiji, and the rest followed. Swamiji said to the disciple on the way, "Shri Ramakrishna has today sat on your head and is blessing you. Take care, never let your mind think of anything transitory, from this day forth." Before crossing a small bridge, Swamiji again said to him, "Beware, now, you must move very cautiously."

Thus all safely reached the Math and rejoiced. Swamiji now entered into a conversation with the disciple, in the course of which he said, "Through the will of Shri Ramakrishna, his Dharmakshetra — sanctified spot — has been established today. A twelve years' anxiety is off my head. Do you know what I am thinking of at this moment? — This Math will be a center of learning and spiritual discipline. Householders of a virtuous turn like yourselves will build houses on the surrounding land and live there, and Sannyasins, men of renunciation, will live in the center, while on that plot of land on the south of the Math, buildings will be erected for English and American disciples to live in. How do you like this idea?

Disciple: Sir, it is indeed a wonderful fancy of yours.

Swamiji: A fancy do you call it? Not at all, everything will come about in time. I am but laying the foundation. There will be lots of further developments in future. Some portion of it I shall live to work out. And I shall infuse into you fellows various ideas, which you will work out in future. It will not do merely to listen to great principles. You must apply them in the practical field, turn them into constant practice. What will be the good of cramming the high-sounding dicta of the scriptures? You have first to grasp the teachings of the Shastras, and then to work them out in practical life. Do you understand? This is called practical religion.

Thus the talk went on, and gradually drifted to the topic of Shankarâchârya. The disciple was a great adherent of Shankara, almost to the point of fanaticism. He used to look upon Shankara's Advaita philosophy as the crest of all philosophies and could not bear any criticism of him. Swamiji was aware of this, and, as was his wont, wanted to break this one-sidedness of the disciple.

Swamiji: Shankara's intellect was sharp like the razor. He was a good arguer and a scholar, no doubt of that, but he had no great liberality; his heart too seems to have been like that. Besides, he used to take great pride in his Brahmanism — much like a southern Brahmin of the priest class, you may say. How he has defended in his commentary on the Vedanta-Sutras that the non-Brahmin castes will not attain to a supreme knowledge of Brahman! And what specious arguments! Referring to Vidura he has said that he became a knower of Brahman by reason of his Brahmin body in the previous incarnation. Well, if nowadays any Shudra attains to a knowledge of Brahman, shall we have to side with your Shankara and maintain that because he had been a Brahmin in his previous birth, therefore he has attained to this knowledge? Goodness! What is the use of dragging in Brahminism with so much ado? The Vedas have entitled any one belonging to the three upper castes to study the Vedas and the realisation of Brahman, haven't they? So Shankara had no need whatsoever of displaying this curious bit of pedantry on this subject, contrary to the Vedas. And such was his heart that he burnt to death lots of Buddhist monks — by defeating them in argument! And the Buddhists, too, were foolish enough to burn themselves to death, simply because they were worsted in argument! What can you call such an action on Shankara's part except fanaticism? But look at Buddha's heart! — Ever ready to give his own life to save the life of even a kid — what to speak of "बहुजनहिताय बहुजनसुखाय — For the welfare of the many, for the happiness of the many"! See, what a large-heartedness — what a compassion!

Disciple: Can't we call that attitude of the Buddha, too, another kind of fanaticism, sir? He went to the length of sacrificing his own body for the sake of a beast!

Swamiji: But consider how much good to the world and its beings came out of that 'fanaticism' of his — how many monasteries and schools and colleges, how many public hospitals and veterinary refuges were established, how developed architecture became — think of that. What was there in this country before Buddha's advent? Only a number of religious principles recorded on bundles of palm leaves — and those too known only to a few. It was Lord Buddha who brought them down to the practical field and showed how to apply them in the everyday life of the people. In a sense, *he* was the living embodiment of true Vedanta.

Disciple: But, sir, it was he who by breaking down the Varnâshrama Dharma (duty according to caste and order of life) brought about a revolution within the fold of Hinduism in India, and there seems to be some truth also in the remark that the religion he preached was for this reason banished in course of time from the soil of India.

Swamiji: It was not through his teachings that Buddhism came to such degradation, it was the fault of his followers. By becoming too philosophic they lost much of their breadth of heart. Then gradually the corruption known as Vâmâchâra (unrestrained mixing with women in the name of religion) crept in and ruined Buddhism. Such diabolical rites are not to be met with in any modern Tantra! One of the principal centres of Buddhism was Jagannâtha or Puri, and you have simply to go there and look at the abominable figures carved on the temple walls to be convinced of this. Puri has come under the sway of the Vaishnavas since the time of Râmânuja and Shri Chaitanya. Through the influence of great personages like these the place now wears an altogether different aspect.

Disciple: Sir, the Shastras tell us of various special influences attaching to places of pilgrimage. How far is this claim true?

Swamiji: When the whole world is the Form Universal of the Eternal Atman, the Ishvara (God), what is there to wonder at in special influences attaching to particular places? There are places where He manifests Himself specially, either spontaneously or through the earnest longing of pure souls, and the ordinary man, if he visits those places with eagerness, attains his end quite easily. Therefore it may lead to the development of the Self in time to have recourse to holy places. But know it for certain that there is no greater Tirtha (holy spot) than the body of man. Nowhere else is the Atman so manifest as here. That car of Jagannatha that you see is but a concrete symbol of this corporeal car. You have to behold the Atman in this car of the body. Haven't you read "आत्मानं रथिनं विद्धि — Know the Atman to be seated on the chariot" etc., "मध्ये वामनमासीनं विश्वे देवा उपासते — All the gods worship the Vâmana (the Supreme Being in a diminutive form) seated in the interior of the body"? The sight of the Atman is the real vision of Jagannatha. And the statement " रथे च वामनं दृष्ट्वा पुनर्जन्म न विद्यते – Seeing the Vâmana on the car, one is no more subject to rebirth", means that if you can visualise the Atman which is within you, and disregarding which you are always identifying yourself with this curious mass of matter, this body of yours — if you can see that, then there is no more rebirth for you. If the sight of the Lord's image on a wooden framework confers liberation on people, then crores of them would be liberated every year — specially with such facility of communication by rail nowadays! But I do not mean to say that the notion which devotees in general entertain towards Shri Jagannatha is either nothing or erroneous. There is a class of people who gradually rise to higher and higher truths with the help of that image. So it is an undoubted fact that in and through that image there is a special manifestation of the Lord.

Disciple: Sir, are there different religions then for the ignorant and the wise?

Swamiji: Quite so. Otherwise why do your scriptures go to such lengths over the specification of the qualifications of an aspirant? All is truth no doubt, but relative truth, different in degrees. Whatever man knows to be truth is of a like nature: some are lesser truths, others, higher ones in comparison with them, while the Absolute Truth is God alone. This Atman is altogether dormant in matter; in man, designated as a living being, It is partially conscious; while in personages like Shri Krishna, Buddha, and Shankara the same Atman has reached the superconscious stage. There is a state even beyond that, which cannot be expressed in terms of thought or language — आवाङ्मनसो गोचरम् ।

Disciple: Sir, there are certain Bhakti sects who hold that we must practise devotion by placing ourselves in a particular attitude or relation with God. They do not understand anything about the glory of the Atman and so forth, and exclusively recommend this constant devotional attitude.

Swamiji: What they say is true to their own case. By continued practice along this line, they too shall feel an awakening of Brahman within them. And what we (Sannyasins) are doing is another kind of practice. We have renounced the world. So how will it suit us to practise by putting ourselves in some worldly relation — such as that of mother, or father, or wife or son, and so forth — with God? To us all these ideals appear to be narrow. Of course it is very difficult to qualify for the worship of God in His absolute, unconditioned aspect. But must we go in for poison because we get no nectar? Always talk and hear and reason about this Atman. By continuing to practise in this way, you will find in time that the Lion (Brahman) will wake up in you too. Go beyond all those relative attitudes — mere sports of the mind. Listen to what Yama says in the Katha Upanisad: उत्तिष्ठत जाग्रत प्राप्य वरान्निबोधत । (Arise, awake, and learn by approaching the élite.) Arise! Awake! and stop not until the goal is reached!

Here the subject was brought to a close. The bell for taking Prasâda (consecrated food) rang, and Swamiji went to partake of it, followed by the disciple.

III

(From the Diary of a Disciple (Shri Sharat Chandra Chakravarty, B.A.))

(Translated from Bengali)

[Place: The rented Math premises at Belur. Time: February, 1898.]

Swamiji has removed the Math from Alambazar to Nilambar Babu's garden at Belur. He is very glad to have come to these new premises. He said to the disciple when the latter came, "See how the Ganga flows by and what a nice building! I like this place. This is the ideal kind of place for a Math." It was then afternoon.

In the evening the disciple found Swamiji alone in the upper storey, and the talk went on, on various topics, in the course of which he wanted to know about Swamiji's boyhood days. Swamiji began to say, "From my very boyhood I was a dare-devil sort of fellow. Otherwise, do you think I could make a tour round the world without a single copper in my pocket?"

In boyhood Swamiji had a great predilection for hearing the chanting of the Râmâyana by professional singers. Wherever such chanting would take place in the neighborhood, he would attend it, leaving sport and all. Swamiji related how, while listening to the Ramayana, on some days, he would be so deeply engrossed in it as to forget all about home, and would have no idea that it was late at night, and that he must return home, and so forth. One day during the chant he heard that the monkey-god Hanumân lived in banana orchards. Forthwith he was so much convinced that when the chant was over, he did not go home straight that night, but loitered in a banana orchard close to his house, with the hope of catching sight of Hanuman, till it was very late in the night.

In his student life he used to pass the day-time only in playing and gambolling with his mates, and study at night bolting the doors. And none could know when he prepared his lessons.

The disciple asked, "Did you see any visions, sir, during your school-days?"

Swamiji: While at school, one night I was meditating within closed doors and had a fairly deep concentration of mind. How long I meditated in that way, I cannot say. It was over, and I still kept my seat, when from the southern wall of that room a luminous figure stepped out and stood in front of me. There was a wonderful radiance on its visage, yet there seemed to be no play of emotion on it. It was the figure of a Sannyasin absolutely calm, shaven-headed, and staff and Kamandalu (a Sannyasin's wooden water-bowl) in hand. He gazed at me for some time and seemed as if he would address me. I too gazed at him in speechless wonder. Then a kind of fright seized me, I opened the door, and hurried out of the room. Then it struck me that it was foolish of me to run away like that, that perhaps he might say something to me. But I have never met that figure since. Many a time and often I have thought that if again I saw him, I would no more be afraid but would speak to him. But I met him no more.

Disciple: Did you ever think on the matter afterwards?

Swamiji: Yes, but I could find no clue to its solution. I now think it was the Lord Buddha whom I saw.

After a short pause, Swamiji said, "When the mind is purified, when one is free from the attachment for lust and gold, one sees lots of visions, most wonderful ones! But one should not pay heed to them. The aspirant cannot advance further if he sets his mind constantly on them. Haven't you heard that Shri Ramakrishna used to say, 'Countless jewels lie uncared for in the outer courts of my beloved Lord's sanctum'? We must come face to face with the Atman; what is the use of setting one's mind on vagaries like those?"

After saying these words, Swamiji sat silent for a while, lost in thought over something. He then resumed:

"Well, while I was in America I had certain wonderful powers developed in me. By looking into people's eyes I could fathom in a trice the contents of their minds. The workings of everybody's mind would be potent to me, like a fruit on the palm of one's hand. To some I used to give out these things, and of those to whom I communicated these, many would become my disciples; whereas those who came to mix with me with some ulterior motive would not, on coming across this power of mine, even venture into my presence any more.

"When I began lecturing in Chicago and other cities, I had to deliver every week some twelve or fifteen or even more lectures at times. This excessive strain on the body and mind would exhaust me to a degree. I seemed to run short of subjects for lectures and was anxious where to find new topics for the morrow's lecture. New thoughts seemed altogether scarce. One day, after the lecture, I lay thinking of what means to adopt next. The thought induced a sort of slumber, and in that state I heard as if somebody standing by me was lecturing — many new ideas and new veins of thought, which I had scarcely heard or thought of in my life. On awaking I remembered them and reproduced them in my lecture. I cannot enumerate how often this phenomenon took place. Many, many days did I hear such lectures while lying in bed. Sometimes the lecture would be delivered in such a loud voice that the inmates of adjacent rooms would hear the sound and ask me the next day, "With whom, Swamiji, were you talking so loudly last night?" I used to avoid the question somehow. Ah, it was a wonderful phenomenon."

The disciple was wonder-struck at Swamiji's words and after thinking deeply on the matter said, "Sir, then you yourself must have lectured like that in your subtle body, and sometimes it would be echoed by the gross body also."

Swamiji listened and replied, "Well, may be."

The topic of his American experiences came up. Swamiji said, "In that country the women are more learned than men. They are all well versed in science and philosophy, and that is why they would appreciate and honour me so much. The men are grinding all day at their work and have very little leisure, whereas the women, by studying and teaching in schools and colleges, have become highly learned. Whichever side you turn your eyes in America, you see the power and influence of women."

Disciple: Well, sir, did not the bigoted Christians oppose you?

Swamiji: Yes, they did. When people began to honour me, then the Padris were after me. They spread many slanders about me by publishing them in the newspapers. Many asked me to contradict these slanders. But I never took the slightest notice of them. It is my firm conviction that no great work is accomplished in this world by low cunning; so without paying any heed to these vile slanders, I used to work steadily at my mission. The upshot I used to find was that often my slanderers, feeling repentant afterwards, would surrender to me and offer apologies, by themselves contradicting the slanders in the papers. Sometimes it so happened that learning that I had been invited to a certain house, somebody would communicate those slanders to my host, who hearing them, would leave home, locking his door. When I went there to attend the invitation, I found it was deserted and nobody was there. Again a few days afterwards, they themselves, learning the truth, would feel sorry for their previous conduct and come to offer themselves as disciples. The fact is, my son, this whole world is full of mean ways of worldliness. But men of real moral courage and discrimination are never deceived by these. Let the world say what it chooses, I shall tread the path of duty – know this to be the line of action for a hero. Otherwise, if one has to attend day and night to what this man says or that man writes, no great work is achieved in this world. Do you know this Sanskrit Shloka: "Let those who are versed in the ethical codes praise or blame, let Lakshmi, the goddess of Fortune, come or go wherever she wisheth, let death overtake him today or after a century, the wise man never swerves from the path of rectitude." (Bhartrihari's Nitishataka) Let people praise you or blame you, let fortune smile or frown upon you, let your body fall today or after a Yuga, see that you do not deviate from the path of Truth. How much of tempest and waves one has to weather, before one reaches the haven of Peace! The greater a man has become, the fiercer ordeal he has had to pass through. Their lives have been tested true by the touchstone of practical life, and only then have they been acknowledged great by the world. Those who are faint-hearted and cowardly sink their barks near the shore, frightened by the raging of waves on the sea. He who is a hero never casts a glance at these. Come what may, I must attain my ideal first – this is Purushakâra, manly endeavour; without such manly endeavor no amount of Divine help will be of any avail to banish your inertia.

Disciple: Is, then, reliance on Divine help a sign of weakness?

Swamiji: In the Shastras real self-surrender and reliance on God has been indicated as the culmination of human achievement. But in your country nowadays the way people speak of Daiva or reliance on Divine dispensation is a sign of death, the outcome of great cowardliness; conjuring up some monstrous idea of God-head and trying to saddle that with all your faults and shortcomings. Haven't you heard Shri Ramakrishna's story about "the sin of killing a cow"? In the end the owner of the garden had to suffer for the sin of killing the cow. Nowadays everybody says: "I am acting as I am being directed by the Lord", and thus throws the burden of both his sins and virtues on the Lord. As if he is himself the lotus-leaf in the water (untouched by it)! If everybody can truly live always in this mood, then he is a Free Soul. But what really happens is that for the "good" I have the credit, but the "bad" Thou, God, art responsible! Praise be to such reliance on God! Without the attainment of the fullness of Knowledge or Divine Love, such a state of absolute reliance on the Lord does not come. He who is truly and sincerely reliant on the Lord goes beyond all idea of the duality of good and bad. The brightest example of the attainment of this state among us at the present time is Nâg Mahâshaya. (Durgâ Charan Nag, a disciple of Shri Ramakrishna.)

Then the conversation drifted to the subject of Nâg Mahâshaya. Swamiji said, "One does not find a second devoted Bhakta like him — Oh, when shall I see him again!"

Disciple: He will soon come to Calcutta to meet you, so mother (Nag Mahashaya's wife) has written to me.

Swamiji: Shri Ramakrishna used to compare him to King Janaka. A man with such control over all the senses one does not hear of even, much less come across. You must associate with him as much as you can. He is one of Shri Ramakrishna's nearest disciples.

Disciple: Many in our part of the country call him a madcap. But I have known him to be a great soul since the very first day of my meeting him. He loves me much, and I have his fervent blessings.

Swamiji: Since you have attained the company of such a Mahâpurusha (holy soul), what more have you to fear about? As an effect of many lives of Tapasyâ one is blessed with the company of such a great soul. How does he live at home?

Disciple: Sir, he has got no business or anything of the kind. He is always busy in serving the guests who come to his house. Beyond the small sum the Pal Babus give him, he has no other means of subsistence; his expenses, however, are like those in a rich family. But he does not spend a pice for his own enjoyment, all that expense is for the service of others. Service — service of others — this seems to be the great mission of his life. It sometimes strikes me that realising the Atman in all creatures, he is engrossed in serving the whole world as a part and parcel of himself. In the service of others he works incessantly and is not conscious even of his body. I suppose, he always lives on the plane which you, sir, call the superconscious state of the mind.

Swamiji: Why should not that be? How greatly was he beloved of Shri Ramakrishna! In your East Bengal, one of Shri Ramakrishna's divine companions has been born in the person of Nag Mahashaya. By his radiance Eastern Bengal has become effulgent.

IV

(From the Diary of a Disciple (Shri Sharat Chandra Chakravarty, B.A.))

(Translated from Bengali)

[Place: The rented Math Premises at Belur. Year: 1898, November.]

It is two or three days since Swamiji has returned from Kashmir. His health is indifferent. When the disciple came to the Math, Swami Brahmananda said, "Since returning from Kashmir, Swamiji does not speak to anybody, he sits in one place rapt in thought; you go to him and by conversation try to draw his mind a little towards worldly objects."

The disciple coming to Swamiji's room in the upper storey found him sitting as if immersed in deep mediation. There was no smile on his face, his brilliant eyes had no outward look, as if intent on seeing something within. Seeing the disciple, he only said, "You have come, my son? Please take your seat", and lapsed into silence. The disciple seeing the inside of his left eye reddened asked, "How is it that your eye is red?" "That is nothing", said Swamiji and was again silent. When even after along time Swamiji did not speak, the disciple was a little troubled at heart and touching his feet said, "Won't you relate to me what things you have seen at Amarnath?" By the disciple's touching his feet, the tensity of his mood was broken a little, as if his attention was diverted a little outwards. He said, "Since visiting Amarnath, I feel as if Shiva is sitting on my head for twenty-four hours and would not come down." The disciple heard it with speechless wonder.

Swamiji: I underwent great religious austerities at Amarnath and then in the temple of Kshir Bhavâni. Go and prepare me some tobacco, I will relate everything to you.

The disciple joyfully obeyed the order. Swamiji slowly smoking began to say, "On the way to Amarnath, I made a very steep ascent on the mountain. Pilgrims do not generally travel by that path. But the determination came upon me that I must go by that path, and so I did. The labour of the strenuous ascent has told on my body. The cold there is so biting that you feel it like pin-pricks."

Disciple: I have heard that it is the custom to visit the image of Amarnath naked; is it so?

Swamiji: Yes, I entered the cave with only my Kaupina on and my body smeared with holy ash; I did not then feel any cold or heat. But when I came out of the temple, I was benumbed by the cold.

Disciple: Did you see the holy pigeons? I have heard, in that cold no living creatures are found to live, but a flight of pigeons from some unknown place frequents the place occasionally.

Swamiji: Yes, I saw three or four white pigeons; whether they live in the cave or the neighboring hills, I could not ascertain.

Disciple: Sir, I have heard people say that the sight of pigeons on coming out of the temple indicates that one has really been blessed with the vision of Shiva.

Swamiji: I have heard that the sight of the pigeons brings to fruition whatever desires one may have.

Then Swamiji said that on the way back he returned to Srinagar by the common route by which the pilgrims return. A few days after returning to Srinagar, he went to visit Kshir Bhavani Devi and staying there for seven days worshipped the Devi and made Homa to her with offerings of Kshira (condensed milk). Every day he used to worship the Devi with a maund of Kshira as offering. One day, while worshipping, the thought arose in Swamiji's mind: "Mother Bhavani has been manifesting Her Presence here for untold years. The Mohammedans came and destroyed her temple, yet the people of the place did nothing to protect Her. Alas, if I were then living I could never have borne it silently." When, thinking in this strain, his mind was much oppressed with sorrow and anguish, he distinctly heard the voice of the Mother saying, "It was according to My desire that the Mohammedans destroyed this temple. It is My desire that I should live in a dilapidated temple, otherwise, can I not immediately erect a seven-storeyed temple of gold here if I like? What can you do? Shall I protect you or shall you protect me!" Swamiji said, "Since hearing that divine voice, I cherish no more plans. The idea of building Maths etc. I have given up; as Mother wills, so it will be." The disciple, speechless with wonder, began to think, "Did he not one day tell me that whatever I saw and heard was but the echo of the Atman within me, that there was nothing outside?" – and fearlessly spoke it out also – "Sir, you used to say that Divine Voices are the echo of our inward thoughts and feelings." Swamiji gravely said, "Whether it be internal or external, if you actually hear with your ears such a disembodied voice, as I have done, can you deny it and call it false? Divine Voices are actually heard, just as you and I are talking."

The disciple, without controverting accepted Swamiji's words, for his words always carried conviction.

He then brought up the subject of departed spirits, and said, "Sir, these ghosts and departed spirits we hear about — which the Shastras also amply corroborate — are all these true or not?

Swamiji: Certainly they are true. Whatever you don't see, are they all false for that? Beyond your sight, millions of universes are revolving at great distances. Because you do not see them, are they non-existent for that? But then, do not put your mind on these subjects of ghosts and spirits. Your mental attitude towards them should be one of indifference. You duty is to realise the Atman within this body. When you realise the Atman, ghosts and spirits will be your slaves.

Disciple: But sir, I think that, if one sees them, it strengthens one's belief in the hereafter, and dispels all doubts about it.

Swamiji: You are heroes; do you mean to say that even you shall have to strengthen your belief in the hereafter by seeing ghosts and spirits! You have read so many sciences and scriptures — have mastered so many secrets of this infinite universe — even with such knowledge, you have to acquire the knowledge of the Atman by seeing ghosts and spirits! What a shame!

Disciple: Well, sir, have you ever seen ghosts and spirits?

Swamiji narrated that a certain deceased relative of his used to come to him as a disembodied spirit. Sometimes it used to bring him information about distant events. But on verification, some of its information was not found to be correct. Afterwards at a certain place of pilgrimage Swamiji prayed for it mentally, wishing it might be released — since then he did not see it again.

The disciple then questioned Swamiji if Shrâddha or other obsequial ceremonies appeased the departed spirits in any way. Swamiji replied, "That is not impossible." On the disciple's asking for the grounds of that belief Swamiji said, "I will explain the subject to you at length some day. There are irrefutable arguments to prove that the Shrâddha ceremony appeases the departed beings. Today I don't feel well. I shall explain it to you another day." But the disciple did not get another opportunity to ask that question to Swamiji.

V

(From the Diary of a Disciple (Shri Sharat Chandra Chakravarty, B.A.))

(Translated from Bengali)

[Place: The rented Math premises at Belur. Year: 1898, November.]

The Math is still situated in Nilambar Babu's garden house at Belur. It is the month of November. Swamiji is now much engaged in the study and discussion of Sanskrit scriptures. The couplet beginning with "*Âchandâlâ-pratihatarayah*", he composed about this time. Today Swamiji composed the hymn, "*Om Hring Ritam*" etc., and handing it over to the disciple said, "See if there is any metrical defect in these stanzas." The disciple made a copy of the poem for this purpose.

On this day it seemed as if the goddess of learning had manifested herself on his tongue. With the disciple he fluently talked about two hours at a stretch in exceedingly melodious Sanskrit. After the disciple had copied the hymn, Swamiji said, "You see, as I write immersed in thought, grammatical slips sometimes occur; therefore I ask you all to look over them."

Disciple: Sir, these are not slips, but the licence of genius.

Swamiji: You may say so; but why will other people assent to that? The other day I wrote an essay on "What is Hinduism", and some amongst you even are complaining that it was written in a very stiff Bengali. I think, language and thought also, like all other things, become lifeless and monotonous in course of time. Such a state seems to have happened now in this country. On the advent of Shri Ramakrishna, however, a new current has set in, in thought and language. Everything has now to be recast in new moulds. Everything has to be propagated with the stamp of new genius. Look, for example, how the old modes of Sannyasins are breaking, yielding place to a new mould by degrees. Society is protesting much against it – but is it of any avail? Neither are we frightened by that. The Sannyasins of the present day have to go to distant countries for preaching, and if they go in an ash-besmeared, half-nude body like the Sâdhus (holy men) of old, in the first place they won't be taken on board the ships, and even if they anyhow reach foreign countries in that dress, they will have to stay in jail. Everything requires to be changed a little according to place, time, and civilisation. Henceforth I am thinking of writing essays in Bengali. Littérateurs will perhaps rail at them. Never mind — I shall try to cast the Bengali language in a new mould. Nowadays, Bengali writers use too many verbs in their writings; this takes away the force of the language. If one can express the ideas of verbs with adjectives, it adds to the force of the language; henceforth try to write in that style. Try to write articles in that style in the *Udbodhan*. Do you know the meaning of the use of verbs in language? It gives a pause to the thought; hence the use of too many verbs in language is the sign of weakness, like quick breathing, and indicates that there is not much vitality in the language; that is why one cannot lecture well in the Bengali language. He who has control over his language, does not make frequent breaks in his thoughts. As your physique has been rendered languid by living on a dietary of boiled rice and *dâl*, similar is the case with your language. In food, in modes of life, in thought, and in language, energy has to be infused. With the infusion of vitality all round and the circulation of blood in all arteries and veins, one should feel the throbbing of new life in everything — then only will the people of this land be able to survive the present terrible struggle for existence; otherwise the country and the race will vanish in the enveloping shadows of death at no distant date.

Disciple: Sir, the constitution of the people of this country has been moulded in a peculiar way through long ages. Is it possible to change that within a short time?

Swamiji: If you have known the old ways to be wrong, then why don't you, as I say, learn to live in a better way? By your example ten other people will follow suit, and by theirs another fifty people will learn. By this process in course of time the new idea will awaken in the hearts of the whole race. But even if after understanding, you do not act accordingly, I shall know that you are wise in words only — but practically you are fools.

Disciple: Your words, sir, infuse great courage, enthusiasm, energy and strength into the heart.

Swamiji: By degrees the heart has to be strengthened. If one man is made, it equals the result of a hundred thousand lectures. Making the mind and lips at one, the ideas have to be practised in life. This is what Shri Ramakrishna meant by "allowing no theft in the chamber of thought". You have to be practical in all spheres of work. The whole country has been ruined by masses of theories. He who is the true son of Shri Ramakrishna will manifest the practical side of religious ideas and will set to work with one-pointed devotion without paying heed to the prattling of men or of society. Haven't you heard of the couplet of Tulsidas: "The elephant walks the market-place and a thousand curs bark at him; so the Sadhus have no ill-feeling if worldly people slander them." You have to walk in this way. No count should be taken of the words of people. If one has to pay heed to their praise or blame, no great work can be accomplished in this life. "

— The Atman is not to be gained by the weak." If there is no strength in the body and mind, the Atman cannot be realised. First you have to build the body by good nutritious food — then only will the mind be strong. The mind is but the subtle part of the body. You must retain great strength in your mind and words. "I am low, I am low" — repeating these ideas in the mind, man belittles and degrades himself. Therefore, the Shastra (*Ashtâvakra Samhita*, I. 11) says:

मुक्ताभिमानी मुक्तो हि बद्धो बद्धाभिमान्यपि ।
किम्वदन्तीह सत्येयं या मतिः सा गतिर्भवेत् ॥

— He who thinks himself free, free he becomes; he who thinks himself bound, bound he remains — this popular saying is true: 'As one thinks, so one becomes'." He alone who is always awake to the idea of freedom, becomes free; he who thinks he is bound, endures life after life in the state of bondage. It is a fact. This truth holds good both in spiritual and temporal matters. Those who are always down-hearted and dispirited in this life can do no work; from life to life they come and go wailing and moaning. "The earth is enjoyed by heroes" — this is the unfailing truth. Be a hero. Always say, "I have no fear." Tell this to everybody — "Have no fear". Fear is death, fear is sin, fear is hell, fear is unrighteousness, fear is wrong life. All the negative thoughts and ideas that are in this world have proceeded from this evil spirit of fear. This fear alone has kept the sun, air and death in their respective places and functions, allowing none to escape from their bounds. Therefore the Shruti says (Katha Upanishad, II. iii, 3) says:

भयादस्याग्निस्तपति भयात्तपति सूर्यः ।
भयादिन्द्रश्च वायुश्च मृत्युर्धावति पञ्चमः ॥

— Through fear of this, fire burns, the sun heats; through fear Indra and Vâyu are carrying on their functions, and Death stalks upon this earth." When the gods Indra, Chandra, Vayu, Varuna will attain to fearlessness, then will they be one with Brahman, and all this phantasm of the world will vanish. Therefore I say, "Be fearless, be fearless,"

Swamiji, in saying these words, appeared in the eyes of the disciple like the very embodiment of "fearlessness", and he thought, "How in his presence even the fear of death leaves one and vanishes into nothingness!"

Swamiji continued: In this embodied existence, you will be tossed again and again on the waves of happiness and misery, prosperity and adversity – but know them all to be of momentary duration. Never care for them. "I am birthless, the deathless Atman, whose nature is Intelligence" – implanting this idea firmly in your heart, you should pass the days of your life. "I have no birth, no death, I am the Atman untouched by anything" – lose yourself completely in this idea. If you can once become one with this idea, then in the hour of sorrow and tribulation, it will rise of itself in your mind, and you will not have to strive with difficulty to bring it up. The other day, I was a guest of Babu Priyanath Mukherjee at Baidyanath. There I had such a spell of asthma that I felt like dying. But from within, with every breath arose the deep-toned sound, "I am He, I am He". Resting on the pillow, I was waiting for the vital breath to depart, and observing all the time that from within was being heard the sound of "I am He, I am He!" I could hear all along "एकमेवाद्वयं ब्रह्म नेह नानास्ति किञ्चन

– The Brahman, the One without a second, alone exists, nothing manifold exists in the world."

The disciple, struck with amazement said, "Sir, talking with you and listening to your realisations, I feel no necessity for the study of scriptures."

Swamiji: No! Scriptures have to be studied also. For the attainment of Jnana, study of scriptures is essential. I shall soon open classes in the Math for them. The Vedas, Upanishads, the Gita, and *Bhâgavata* should be studied in the classes, and I shall teach the Pânini's *Ashtâdhyâyai*.

Disciple: Have you studied the *Ashtadhayayi* of Panini?

Swamiji: When I was in Jaipur, I met a great grammarian and felt a desire to study Sanskrit grammar with him. Although he was a great scholar in that branch, he had not much aptitude for teaching. He explained to me the commentary on the first aphorism for three days continuously, still I could not grasp a bit of it. On the fourth day the teacher got annoyed and said, "Swamiji, I could not make you understand the meaning of the first aphorism even in three days; I fear, you will not be much benefited by my teaching." Hearing these words, a great self-reproach came over me. Putting food and sleep aside, I set myself to study the commentary on the first aphorism independently. Within three hours the sense of the commentary stood explained before me as clearly as anything; then going to my teacher I gave him the sense of the whole commentary. My teacher, hearing me, said, "How could you gather the sense so excellently within three hours, which I failed to explain to you in three days?" After that, every day I began to read chapter after chapter, with the greatest ease. Through concentration of mind everything can be accomplished — even mountains can be crushed to atoms.

Disciple: Sir, everything is wonderful about you.

Swamiji: There is nothing wonderful in this universe. Ignorance constitutes the only darkness, which confers all things and makes them look mysterious. When everything is lighted by Knowledge, the sense of mystery vanishes from the face of things. Even such an inscrutable thing as Maya, which brings the most impossible things to pass, disappears. Know Him, think of Him, by knowing whom everything else is known. And when that Atman is realised, the purport of all scriptures will be perceived as clearly as a fruit on the palm of one's hand. The Rishis of old attained realisation, and must we fail? We are also men. What has happened once in the life of one individual must, through proper endeavour, be realised in the life of others. History repeats itself. This Atman is the same in all, there is only a difference of manifestation in different individuals. Try to manifest this Atman, and you will see your intellect penetrating into all subjects. The intellect of one who has not realised the Atman is one-sided, whereas the genius of the knower of Atman is all-embracing. With the manifestation of the Atman you will find that science, philosophy, and everything will be easily mastered. Proclaim the glory of the Atman with the roar of a lion, and impart fearlessness unto all beings by saying, "Arise, awake, and stop not till the goal is reached."

VI

(From the Diary of a Disciple (Shri Sharat Chandra Chakravarty, B.A.))

(Translated from Bengali)

[Place: The rented Math premises at Belur. Year: 1898.]

The disciple is staying with Swamiji at the garden-house of Nilambar Babu at Belur for the last two days.

Today, Swamiji has given permission to the disciple to stay in his room at night. When the disciple was serving Swamiji and massaging his feet, he spoke to him: "What folly! Leaving such a place as this, you want to go back to Calcutta! See what an atmosphere of holiness is here – the pure air of the Ganga – what an assemblage of Sadhus – will you find anywhere a place like this!"

Disciple: Sir, as the fruition of great austerities in past lives, I have been blessed with your company. Now bless me that I may not be overcome by ignorance and delusion any more. Now my mind sometimes is seized with a great longing for some direct spiritual realisation.

Swamiji: I also felt like that many times. One day in the Cossipore garden, I had expressed my prayer to Shri Ramakrishna with great earnestness. Then in the evening, at the hour of meditation, I lost the consciousness of the body, and felt that it was absolutely non-existent. I felt that the sun, moon, space, time, ether, and all had been reduced to a homogeneous mass and then melted far away into the unknown; the body-consciousness had almost vanished, and I had nearly merged in the Supreme. But I had just a trace of the feeling of Ego, so I could again return to the world of relativity from the Samâdhi. In this state of Samadhi all the difference between "I" and the "Brahman" goes away, everything is reduced into unity, like the waters of the Infinite Ocean – water everywhere, nothing else exists – language and thought, all fail there. Then only is the state "beyond mind and speech" realised in its actuality. Otherwise, so long as the religious aspirant thinks or says, "I am the Brahman" – "I" and "the Brahman", these two entities persist – there is the involved semblance of duality. After that experience, even after trying repeatedly, I failed to bring back the state of Samadhi.

On informing Shri Ramakrishna about it, he said, "If you remain day and night in that state, the work of the Divine Mother will not be accomplished; therefore you won't be able to induce that state again; when your work is finished, it will come again."

Disciple: On the attainment of the absolute and transcendent Nirvikalpa Samadhi can none return to the world of duality through the consciousness of Egoism?

Swamiji: Shri Ramakrishna used to say that the Avataras alone can descend to the ordinary plane from that state of Samadhi, for the good of the world. Ordinary Jivas do not; immersed in that state, they remain alive for a period of twenty-one days; after that, their body drops like a sere leaf from the tree of Samsâra (world).

Disciple: When in Samadhi the mind is merged, and there remain no waves on the surface of consciousness, where then is the possibility of mental activity and returning to the world through the consciousness of Ego? When there is no mind, then who will descend from Samadhi to the relative plane, and by what means?

Swamiji: The conclusion of the Vedanta is that when there is absolute samadhi and cessation of all modifications, there is no return from that state; as the Vedanta Aphorism says: "अनावृत्तिः शब्दात् – There is non-return, from scriptural texts." But the Avataras cherish a few desires for the good of the world. By taking hold of that thread, they come down from the superconscious to the conscious state.

Disciple: But, sir, if one or two desires remain, how can that state be called the absolute, transcendent Samadhi? For the scriptures say that in that state all the modifications of the mind and all desires are stamped out.

Swamiji: How then can there be projection of the universe after Mahâpralaya (final dissolution)? At Mahapralaya everything is merged in the Brahman. But even after that, one hears and reads of creation in the scriptures, that projection and contraction (of the universe) go on in wave forms. Like the fresh creation and dissolution of the universe after Mahapralaya, the superconscious and conscious states of Avataras also stand to reason.

Disciple: If I argue that at the time of dissolution the seeds of further creation remain almost merged in Brahman, and that it is not absolute dissolution or Nirvikalpa Samadhi?

Swamiji: Then I shall ask you to answer how the projection of the universe is possible from Brahman in which there is no shadow of any qualification – which is unaffected and unqualified.

Disciple: Why, this is but a seeming projection. The reply to the question is given in the scriptures in this way, that the manifestation of creation from Brahman is only an appearance like the mirage in the desert, but really there has been no creation or anything of the kind. This illusion is produced by Maya, which is the negation of the eternally existing Brahman, and hence unreal.

Swamiji: If the creation is false, then you can also regard the Nirvikalpa Samadhi of Jiva and his return therefrom as seeming appearances. Jiva is Brahman by his nature. How can he have any experience of bondage? Your desire to realise the truth that you are Brahman is also a hallucination in that case — for the scripture says, "You are already that." Therefore, " अयमेव हि ते बन्ध समाधिनमनुतिष्ठसि — This is verily your bondage that you are practising the attainment of Samadhi."

Disciple: This is a great dilemma. If I am Brahman, why don't I always realise it?

Swamiji: In order to attain to that realisation in the conscious plane, some instrumentality is required. The mind is that instrument in us. But it is a non-intelligent substance. It only appears to be intelligent through the light of the Atman behind. Therefore the author of the Panchadashi (III. 40) says: " चिच्छायवेशत: शक्तिश्चेतनेव विभाति सा — The Shakti appears to be intelligent by the reflection of the intelligence of the Atman." Hence the mind also appears to us like an intelligent substance. Therefore it is certain that you won't be able to know the Atman, the Essence of Intelligence, through the mind. You have to go beyond the mind — for only the Atman exists there — there the object of knowledge becomes the same as the instrument of knowledge. The knower, knowledge, and the instrument of knowledge become one and the same. It is therefore that the Shruti says, " विज्ञातारमरे केन विजानीयात् — Through what are you to know the Eternal Subject?" The real fact is that there is a state beyond the conscious plane, where there is no duality of the knower, knowledge, and the instrument of knowledge etc. When the mind is merged, that state is perceived. I say it is "perceived," because there is no other word to express that state. Language cannot express that state. Shankaracharya has styled it "Transcendent Perception" (Aparokshânubhuti). Even after that transcendent perception Avataras descend to the relative plane and give glimpses of that — therefore it is said that the Vedas and other scriptures have originated from the perception of Seers. The case of ordinary Jivas is like that of the salt-doll which attempting to sound the depths of the ocean melted into it. Do you see? The sum and substance of it is — you have only got to know that you are Eternal Brahman.

You are already that, only the intervention of a non-intelligent mind (which is called Maya in the scriptures) is hiding that knowledge. When the mind composed of subtle matter is quelled, the Atman is effulgent by Its own radiance. One proof of the fact that Maya or mind is an illusion is that the mind by itself is non-intelligent and of the nature of darkness; and it is the light of the Atman behind, that makes it appear as intelligent. When you will understand this, the mind will merge in the unbroken Ocean of Intelligence; then you will realise: — This Atman is Brahman."

Then Swamiji, addressing the disciple, said, "You feel sleepy, then go to sleep."

* * *

In the night the disciple had a wonderful dream, as a result of which he earnestly begged Swamiji's permission to worship him. Swamiji had to acquiesce, and after the ceremony was over he said to the disciple, "Well, your worship is finished, but Premananda will be in a rage at your sacrilegious act of worshipping my feet in the flower-tray meant for Shri Ramakrishna's worship." Before his words were finished, Swami Premananda came there, and Swamiji said to him, "See what a sacrilege he has committed! With the requisites of Shri Ramakrishna's worship, he has worshipped me!" Swami Premananda, smiling, said, "Well done! Are you and Shri Ramakrishna different?" — hearing which the disciple felt at ease.

The disciple is an orthodox Hindu. Not to speak of prohibited food, he does not even take food touched by another. Therefore Swamiji sometimes used to refer to him as "priest". Swamiji, while he was eating biscuits with his breakfast, said to Swami Sadananda, "Bring the priest in here." When the disciple came to Swamiji, he gave some portion of his food to him to eat. Finding the disciple accepting it without any demur, Swamiji said, "Do you know what you have eaten now? These are made from eggs." In reply, the disciple said, "Whatever may be in it, I have no need to know; taking this sacramental food from you, I have become immortal."

Thereupon Swamiji said, "I bless you that from this day all your egoism of caste, colour, high birth, religious merit and demerit, and all, may vanish for ever!". . .

VII

(From the Diary of a Disciple (Shri Sharat Chandra Chakravarty, B.A.))

(Translated from Bengali)

[Place: The rented Math premises at Belur. Year: 1898.]

The disciple has come to the Math this morning. As soon as he stood after touching the feet of Swamiji, Swamiji said, "What's the use of your continuing in service any more? Why not go in for some business?" The disciple was then employed as a private tutor in some family. Asked about the profession of teaching, Swamiji said, "If one does the work of teaching boys for a long time, one gets blunt in intellect; one's intelligence is not manifested. If one stays among a crowd of boys day and night, gradually one gets obtuse. So give up the working of teaching boys."

Disciple: What shall I do, then?

Swamiji; Why, if you want to live the life of a worldly man and have a desire for earning money, then go over to America. I shall give you directions for business. You will find that in five years you will get together a lot of money.

Disciple: What business shall I go in for? And where am I to get the money from?

Swamiji: What nonsense are you talking? Within you lies indomitable power. Only thinking, "I am nothing, I am nothing", you have become powerless. Why, you alone! The whole race has become so. Go round the world once, and you will find how vigorously the life-current of other nations is flowing. And what are you doing? Even after learning so much, you go about the doors of others, crying, "Give me employment". Trampled under others' feet doing slavery for others, are you men any more? You are not worth a pin's head! In this fertile country with abundant water-supply, where nature produces wealth and harvest a thousand times more than in others, you have no food for your stomach, no clothes to cover your body! In this country of abundance, the produce of which has been the cause of the spread of civilisation in other countries, you are reduced to such straits! Your condition is even worse than that of a dog. And you glory in your

Vedas and Vedanta! A nation that cannot provide for its simple food and clothing, which always depends on others for its subsistence — what is there for it to vaunt about? Throw your religious observances overboard for the present and be first prepared for the struggle for existence. People of foreign countries are turning out such golden results from the raw materials produced in your country, and you, like asses of burden, are only carrying their load. The people of foreign countries import Indian raw goods, manufacture various commodities by bringing their intelligence to bear upon them, and become great; whereas you have locked up your intelligence, thrown away your inherited wealth to others, and roam about crying piteously for food.

Disciple: In what way, sir, can the means of subsistence be procured?

Swamiji: Why, the means are in your hands. You blindfold your eyes, and say, "I am blind and can see nothing." Tear off the folds from your eyes and you will see the whole world lighted by the rays of the midday sun. If you cannot procure money, go to foreign countries, working your passage as a Lascar. Take Indian cloth, towels, bamboo-work, and other indigenous products, and peddle in the streets of Europe and America; you will find how greatly Indian products are appreciated in foreign markets even now. In America I found, some Mohammedans of the Hooghly district had grown rich by peddling Indian commodities in this way. Have you even less intelligence than they? Take, for example, such excellent fabric as the Varanasi-made Sâris of India, the like of which are not produced anywhere else in the world. Go to America with this cloth. Have gowns made out of this fabric and sell them, and you will see how much you earn.

Disciple: Sir, why will they wear gowns made of the Saris of Varanasi? I have heard that clothes designed diversely are not to the taste of the ladies in those countries.

Swamiji: Whether they will receive or not, I shall look to that. It is for you to exert yourself and go over there. I have many friends in that country, to whom I shall introduce you. At first I shall request them to take this cloth up among themselves. Then you will find many will follow suit, and at last you won't be able to keep the supply up to the enormous demand.

Disciple: Where shall I get the capital for the business?

Swamiji: I shall somehow give you a start; for the rest you must depend on your own exertions. "If you die, you get to heaven; and if you win, you enjoy the earth" (Gita). Even if you die in this attempt, well and good, many will take up the work, following your example. And if you succeed, you will live a life of great opulence.

Disciple: Yes, sir, so it is. But I cannot muster sufficient courage.

Swamiji: That is what I say, my son, you have no Shraddhâ — no faith in yourselves. What will you achieve? You will have neither material nor spiritual advancement. Either put forth your energy in the way I have suggested and be successful in life, or give up all and take to the path we have chosen. Serve the people of all countries through spiritual instruction — then only will you get your dole of food like us. If there is no mutual exchange, do you think anybody cares for anybody else? You observe in our case, that because we give the householders some spiritual instructions, they in return give us some morsels of food. If you do nothing, why will they give you food? You observe so much misery in mere service and slavery of others, still you are not waking up; and so your misery also is never at an end. This is certainly the delusive power of Maya! In the West I have found that those who are in the employment of others have their seats fixed in the back rows in the Parliament, while the front seats are reserved for those who have made themselves famous by self-exertion, or education, or intelligence. In Western countries there is no botheration of caste. Those on whom Fortune smiles for their industry and exertion are alone regarded as leaders of the country and the controllers of its destiny. Whereas in your country, you are simply vaunting your superiority in caste, till at last you cannot even get a morsel of food! You have not the capacity to manufacture a needle, and you dare to criticise the English! Fools! Sit at their feet and learn from them the arts, industries, and the practicality necessary for the struggle for existence. You will be esteemed once more when you will become fit. Then they too will pay heed to your words. Without the necessary preparation, what will mere shouting in the Congress avail?

Disciple: But, sir, all the educated men of the country have joined it.

Swamiji: Well, you consider a man as educated if only he can pass some examinations and deliver good lectures. The education which does not help the common mass of people to equip themselves for the struggle for life, which does not bring out strength of character, a spirit of philanthropy, and the courage of a lion — is it worth the name? Real education is that which enables one to stand on one's own legs. The education that you are receiving now in schools and colleges is only making you a race of dyspeptics. You are working like machines merely, and living a jelly-fish existence.

The peasant, the shoemaker, the sweeper, and such other lower classes of India have much greater capacity for work and self-reliance than you. They have been silently working through long ages and producing the entire wealth of the land, without a word of complaint. Very soon they will get above you in position. Gradually capital is drifting into their hands, and they are not so much troubled with wants as you are. Modern education has changed your fashion, but new avenues of wealth lie yet undiscovered for want of the inventive genius. You have so long oppressed these forbearing masses; now is the time for their retribution. And you will become extinct in your vain search for employment, making it the be-all and end-all of your life.

Disciple: Sir, although our power of originality is less than that of other countries, still the lower classes of India are being guided by our intelligence. So where will they get the power and culture to overcome the higher classes in the struggle for existence?

Swamiji: Never mind if they have not read a few books like you – if they have not acquired your tailor-made civilisation. What do these matter? But they are the backbone of the nation in all countries. If these lower classes stop work, from where will you get your food and clothing? If the sweepers of Calcutta stop work for a day, it creates a panic; and if they strike for three days, the whole town will be depopulated by the outbreak of epidemics. If the labourers stop work, your supply of food and clothes also stops. And you regard them as low-class people and vaunt your own culture!

Engrossed in the struggle for existence, they had not the opportunity for the awakening of knowledge. They have worked so long uniformly like machines guided by human intelligence, and the clever educated section have taken the substantial part of the fruits of their labour. In every country this has been the case. But times have changed. The lower classes are gradually awakening to this fact and making a united front against this, determined to exact their legitimate dues. The masses of Europe and America have been the first to awaken and have already begun the fight. Signs of this awakening have shown themselves in India, too, as is evident from the number of strikes among the lower classes nowadays. The upper classes will no longer be able to repress the lower, try they ever so much. The well-being of the higher classes now lies in helping the lower to get their legitimate rights.

Therefore I say, set yourselves to the task of spreading education among the masses. Tell them and make them understand, "You are our brothers – a part and parcel of our bodies, and we love you and never hate you." If they receive this sympathy from you, their enthusiasm for work will be increased a hundredfold. Kindle their knowledge with the help of modern science. Teach them history, geography, science, literature, and along with these the profound truths of religion. In exchange for that teaching, the poverty of the teachers will also disappear. By mutual exchange both parties will become friendly to each other.

Disciple: But, sir, with the spread of learning among them, they too will in course of time have fertile brains but become idle and inactive like us and live on the fruits of the labour of the next lower classes.

Swamiji: Why shall it be so? Even with the awakening of knowledge, the potter will remain a potter, the fisherman a fisherman, the peasant a peasant. Why should they leave their hereditary calling? " सहजं कर्म कौन्तेय सदोषमपि न त्यजेत् – Don't give up the work to which you were born, even if it be attended with defects." If they are taught in this way, why should they give up their respective callings? Rather they will apply their knowledge to the better performance of the work to which they have been born. A number of geniuses are sure to arise from among them in the course of time. You (the higher classes) will take these into your own fold. The Brahmins acknowledged the valiant king Vishvâmitra as a Brahmin, and think how grateful the whole Kshatriya race became to the Brahmins for this act! By such sympathy and co-operation even birds and beasts become one's own — not to speak of men!

Disciple: Sir, what you say is true, but there yet seems to be a wide gulf between the higher and lower classes. To bring the higher classes to sympathise with the lower seems to be a difficult affair in India.

Swamiji: But without that there is no well-being for your upper classes. You will be destroyed by internecine quarrels and fights — which you have been having so long. When the masses will wake up, they will come to understand your oppression of them, and by a puff of their mouth you will be entirely blown away! It is they who have introduced civilisation amongst you; and it is they who will then pull it down. Think how at the hands of the Gauls the mighty ancient Roman civilisation crumbled into dust! Therefore I say, try to rouse these lower classes from slumber by imparting learning and culture to them. When they will awaken — and awaken one day they must — they also will not forget your good services to them and will remain grateful to you.

After such conversation Swamiji, addressing the disciple, said: Let these subjects drop now — come, tell me what you have decided. Do something, whatever it be. Either go in for some business, or like us come to the path of real Sannyasa, " आत्मनो मोक्षार्थं जगद्धिताय च – For one's own liberation and for the good of the world." The latter path is of course the best way there is. What good will it do to be a worthless householder? You have understood that everything in life is transitory: " नलिनीदलगतजलमतितरलम् तद्वज्जीवनमतिशयचपलम् — Life is as unstable as the water on the lotus leaf." Therefore if you have the enthusiasm for acquiring this knowledge of the Atman, do not wait any more but come forward immediately. " — The very day that you feel dispassion for the world, that very day renounce and take to Sannyasa" (Jâbâlopanishad, 4). Sacrifice your life for the good of others and go round to the doors of people carrying this message of fearlessness "उत्तिष्ठत जाग्रत प्राप्य वरान् निबोधत — Arise, awake, and stop not till the goal is reached."

VIII

(From the Diary of a Disciple (Shri Sharat Chandra Chakravarty, B.A.))

(Translated from Bengali)

[Place: Calcutta. Year: *1898.*]

Swamiji accompanied by Sister Nivedita, Swami Yogananda, and others has come to visit the Zoological Gardens at Alipur in the afternoon. Rai Rambrahma Sanyal Bahadur, Superintendent of the Gardens, cordially received them and took them round the Gardens. Swamiji, as he went on seeing the various species of animals, casually referred to the Darwinian theory of the gradual evolution of animals. The disciple remembers how, entering the room for snakes, he pointed to a huge python with circular rings on its body, with the remark: "From this the tortoise has evolved in course of time. That very snake, by remaining stationary at one spot for a long time, has gradually turned hard-backed." He further said in fun to the disciple, "You eat tortoises, don't you? Darwin holds that it is this snake that has evolved into the tortoise in the process of time – then you eat snakes too!" The disciple protested, "Sir, when a thing is metamorphosed into another thing through evolution, it has no more its former shape and habits; then how can you say that eating tortoise means eating snakes also?"

This answer created laughter among the party. After seeing some other things, Swamiji went to Rambrahma Babu's quarters in the Gardens, where he took tea, and others also did the same. Finding that the disciples hesitated to sit at the same table and partake of the sweets and tea which Sister Nivedita had touched, Swamiji repeatedly urged him to take them, which he was induced to do, and drinking water himself, he gave the rest of it to the disciple to drink. After this there was a short conversation on Darwin's evolution theory.

Rambrahma Babu: What is your opinion of the evolution theory of Darwin and the causes he has put forward for it?

Swamiji: Taking for granted that Darwin is right, I cannot yet admit that it is the final conclusion about the causes of evolution.

Rambrahma Babu: Did the ancient scholars of our country discuss this subject?

Swamiji: The subject has been nicely discussed in the Samkhya Philosophy. I am of opinion that the conclusion of the ancient Indian philosophers is the last word on the causes of evolution.

Rambrahma Babu: I shall be glad to hear of it, if it can be explained in a few words.

Swamiji: You are certainly aware of the laws of struggle for existence, survival of the fittest, natural selection, and so forth, which have been held by the Western scholars to be the causes of elevating a lower species to a higher. But none of these has been advocated as the cause of that in the system of Patanjali. Patanjali holds that the transformation of one species into another is effected by the "in-filling of nature" ( ) It is not that this is done by the constant struggle against obstacles. In my opinion, struggle and competition sometimes stand in the way of a being's attaining its perfection. If the evolution of an animal is effected by the destruction of a thousand others, then one must confess that this evolution is doing very little good to the world. Taking it for granted that it conduces to physical well-being, we cannot help admitting that it is a serious obstacle to spiritual development. According to the philosophers of our country, every being is a perfect Soul, and the diversity of evolution and manifestation of nature is simply due to the difference in the degree of manifestation of this Soul. The moment the obstacles to the evolution and manifestation of nature are completely removed, the Soul manifests Itself perfectly. Whatever may happen in the lower strata of nature's evolutions, in the higher strata at any rate, it is not true that it is only by constantly struggling against obstacles that one has to go beyond them. Rather it is observed that there the obstacles give way and a greater manifestation of the Soul takes place through education and culture, through concentration and meditation, and above all through sacrifice. Therefore, to designate the obstacles not as the effects but as the causes of the Soul-manifestation, and describe them as aiding this wonderful diversity of nature, is not consonant with reason. The attempt to remove evil from the world by killing a thousand evil-doers, only adds to the evil in the world. But if the people can be made to desist from evil-doing by means of spiritual instruction, there is no more evil in the world. Now, see how horrible the Western struggle theory becomes!

Rambrahma Babu was astonished to hear Swamiji's words and said at length, "India badly needs at the present moment men well versed in the Eastern and Western philosophies like you. Such men alone are able to point out the mistakes of the educated people who see only one side of the shield. I am extremely delighted to hear your original explanation of the evolution theory."

Shortly after, Swamiji with the party left for Baghbazar and reached Balaram Bose's house at about 8 p.m. After a short rest, he came to the drawing-room, where there was a small gathering, all eager to hear of the conversation at the Zoological Gardens in detail. When Swamiji came to the room, the disciple, as the spokesman of the meeting, raised that very topic.

Disciple: Sir, I have not been able to follow all your remarks about the evolution theory at the Zoo. Will you kindly recapitulate them in simple words?

Swamiji: Why, which points did you fail to grasp?

Disciple: You have often told us that it is the power to struggle with the external forces which constitutes the sign of life and the first step towards improvement. Today you seem to have spoken just the opposite thing.

Swamiji: Why should I speak differently? It was you who could not follow me. In the animal kingdom we really see such laws as struggle for existence, survival of the fittest, etc., evidently at work. Therefore Darwin's theory seems true to a certain extent. But in the human kingdom, where there is the manifestation of rationality, we find just the reverse of those laws. For instance, in those whom we consider really great men or ideal characters, we scarcely observe any external struggle. In the animal kingdom instinct prevails; but the more a man advances, the more he manifests rationality. For this reason, progress in the rational human kingdom cannot be achieved, like that in the animal kingdom, by the destruction of others! The highest evolution of man is effected through sacrifice alone. A man is great among his fellows in proportion as he can sacrifice for the sake of others, while in the lower strata of the animal kingdom, that animal is the strongest which can kill the greatest number of animals. Hence the struggle theory is not equally applicable to both kingdoms. Man's struggle is in the mental sphere. A man is greater in proportion as he can control his mind. When the mind's activities are perfectly at rest, the Atman manifests Itself. The struggle which we observe in the animal kingdom for the preservation of the gross body obtains in the human plane of existence for gaining mastery over the mind or for attaining the state of balance. Like a living tree and its reflection in the water of a tank, we find opposite kinds of struggle in the animal and human kingdoms.

Disciple: Why then do you advocate so much the improvement of our physique?

Swamiji: Well, do you consider yourselves as men? You have got only a bit of rationality — that's all. How will you struggle with the mind unless the physique be strong? Do you deserve to be called men any longer — the highest evolution in the world? What have you got besides eating, sleeping, and satisfying the creature-comforts? Thank your stars that you have not developed into quadrupeds yet! Shri Ramakrishna used to say, "He is the man who is conscious of his dignity". You are but standing witnesses to the lowest class of insect-like existence of which the scripture speaks, that they simply undergo the round of births and deaths without being allowed to go to any of the higher spheres! You are simply living a life of jealousy among yourselves and are objects of hatred in the eyes of the foreigner. You are animals, therefore I recommend you to struggle. Leave aside theories and all that. Just reflect calmly on your own everyday acts and dealings with others and find out whether you are not a species of beings intermediate between the animal and human planes of existence! First build up your own physique. Then only you can get control over the mind. — This Self is not to be attained by the weak" (Katha Upanishad, I.ii.23).

Disciple: But, sir, the commentator (Shankara) has interpreted the word "weak" to mean "devoid of Brahmacharya or continence".

Swamiji: Let him. I say, "The physically weak are unfit for the realisation of the Self."

Disciple: But many dull-headed persons also have strong bodies.

Swamiji: If you can take the pains to give them good ideas once, they will be able to work them out sooner than physically unfit people. Don't you find that in a weak physique it is difficult to control the sex-appetite or anger? Lean people are quickly incensed and are quickly overcome by the sex-instinct.

Disciple: But we find exceptions to the rule also.

Swamiji: Who denies it? Once a person gets control over the mind, it matters little whether the body remains strong or becomes emaciated. The gist of the thing is that unless one has a good physique one can never aspire to Self-realisation. Shri Ramakrishna used to say, "One fails to attain realisation if there be but a slight defect in the body".

Finding that Swamiji had grown excited, the disciple did not dare to push the topic further, but remained quiet accepting Swamiji's view. Shortly after, Swamiji, addressing those present, said, "By the bye, have you heard that this 'priest' has today taken food which was touched by Nivedita? That he took the sweets touched by her did not matter so much, but — here he addressed the disciple — "how did you drink the water she had touched?"

Disciple: But it was you, sir, who ordered me to do so. Under the Guru's orders I can do anything. I was unwilling to drink the water though. But you drank it and I had to take it as Prasâda.

Swamiji: Well, your caste is gone for ever. Now nobody will respect you as a Brahmin of the priest class.

Disciple: I don't care if they do not. I can take the rice from the house of a Pariah if you order me to.

These words set Swamiji and all those present in a roar of laughter.

The conversation lasted till it was past midnight, when the disciple came back to his lodging, only to find it bolted. So he had to pass the night out of doors.

The wheel of Time has rolled on in its unrelenting course, and Swamiji, Swami Yogananda, and Sister Nivedita are now no more on earth. Only the sacred memory of their lives remains — and the disciple considers himself blessed to be able to record, in ever so meagre a way, these reminiscences.

IX

(From the Diary of a Disciple (Shri Sharat
Chandra Chakravarty, B.A.))
(Translated from Bengali)

[Place: The rented Math premises at Belur. Year: 1898.]

The disciple has come to the Math (monastery) today. It has now been removed to Nilambar Babu's garden-house, and the site of the present Math has recently been purchased. Swamiji is out visiting the new Math-grounds at about four o'clock, taking the disciple with him. The site was then mostly jungle, but on the north side of it there was a one-storeyed brick-built house. Swamiji began to walk over the site and to discuss in the course of conversation the plan of work of the future Math and its rules and regulations.

Reaching by degrees the veranda on the east side of the one-storeyed house, Swamiji said, "Here would be the place for the Sadhus to live. It is my wish to convert this Math into a chief centre of spiritual practices and the culture of knowledge. The power that will have its rise from here will flood the whole world and turn the course of men's lives into different channels; from this place will spring forth ideals which will be the harmony of Knowledge, Devotion, Yoga, and Work; at a nod from the men of this Math a life-giving impetus will in time be given to the remotest corners of the globe; while all true seekers after spirituality will in course of time assemble here. A thousand thoughts like these are arising in my mind.

"Yonder plot of land on the south side of the Math will be the centre of learning, where grammar, philosophy, science, literature, rhetoric, the Shrutis, Bhakti scriptures, and English will be taught. This Temple of Learning will be fashioned after the Tols of old days. Boys who are Brahmacharins from their childhood will live there and study the scriptures. Their food and clothing and all will be supplied from the Math. After a course of five years' training these Brahmacharins may, if they like, go back to their homes and lead householders' lives; or they may embrace the monastic life with the sanction of the venerable Superiors of the Math. The authorities of the Math will have the power to turn out at once any of these Brahmacharins who will be found refractory or of a bad character. Teaching will be imparted here irrespective of caste or creed, and those who will have objection to this will not be admitted. But those who would like to observe their particular caste-rites, should make separate arrangements for their food, etc. They will only attend the classes along with the rest. The Math authorities shall keep a vigilant watch over the character of these also. None but those that are trained here shall be eligible for Sannyasa. Won't it be nice when by degrees this Math will begin to work like this?"

Disciple: Then you want to reintroduce into the country the ancient institution of living a Brahmacharin's life in the house of the Guru?

Swamiji: Exactly. The modern system of education gives no facility for the development of the knowledge of Brahman. We must found Brahmacharya Homes as in times of old. But now we must lay their foundations on a broad basis, that is to say, we must introduce a good deal of change into it to suit the requirements of the times. Of this I shall speak to you later on.

"That piece of land to the south of the Math," Swamiji resumed, "we must also purchase in time. There we shall start an Annasatra – a Feeding Home. There arrangements will be made for serving really indigent people in the spirit of God. The Feeding Home will be named after Shri Ramakrishna. Its scope will at first be determined by the amount of funds. For the matter of that, we may start it with two or three inmates. We must train energetic Brahmacharins to conduct this Home. They will have to collect the funds for its maintenance – ay, even by begging. The Math will not be allowed to give any pecuniary help in this matter. The Brahmacharins themselves shall have to raise funds for it. Only after completing their five years' training in this Home of Service, will they be allowed to join the Temple of Learning branch. After a training of ten years – five in the Feeding Home and five in the Temple of Learning – they will be allowed to enter the life of Sannyasa, having initiation from the Math authorities – provided of course they have a mind to become Sannyasins and the Math authorities consider them fit for Sannyasa and are willing to admit them into it. But the Head of the Math will be free to confer Sannyasa on any exceptionally meritorious Brahmacharin, at any time, in defiance of this rule. The ordinary Brahmacharins, however, will have to qualify themselves for Sannyasa by degrees, as I have just said. I have all these ideas in my brain."

Disciple: Sir, what will be the object of starting three such sections in the Math?

Swamiji: Didn't you understand me? First of all, comes the gift of food; next is the gift of learning, and the highest of all is the gift of knowledge. We must harmonise these three ideals in the Math. By continuously practising the gift of food, the Brahmacharins will have the idea of practical work for the sake of others and that of serving all beings in the spirit of the Lord firmly impressed on their minds. This will gradually purify their minds and lead to the manifestation of Sâttvika (pure and unselfish) ideas. And having this the Brahmacharins will in time acquire the fitness for attaining the knowledge of Brahman and become eligible for Sannyasa.

Disciple: Sir, if, as you say, the gift of (spiritual) knowledge is the highest, why then start sections for the gift of food and the gift of learning?

Swamiji: Can't you understand this point even now? Listen. If in these days of food scarcity you can, for the disinterested service of others, get together a few morsels of food by begging or any other means, and give them to the poor and suffering, that will not only be doing good to yourself and the world, but you will at the same time get everybody's sympathy for this noble work. The worldly-minded people, tied down to lust and wealth, will have faith in you for this labour of love and come forward to help you. You will attract a thousand times as many men by this unasked-for gift of food, as you will by the gift of learning or of (spiritual) knowledge. In no other work will you get so much public sympathy as you will in this. In a truly noble work, not to speak of men, even God Himself befriends the doer. When people have thus been attracted, you will be able to stimulate the desire for learning and spirituality in them. Therefore the gift of food comes first.

Disciple; Sir, to start Feeding Homes we want a site first, then buildings, and then the funds to work them. Where will so much money come from?

Swamiji: The southern portion of the Math premises I am leaving at your disposal immediately, and I am getting a thatched house erected under that Bael tree. You just find out one or two blind or infirm people and apply yourself to their service. Go and beg food for them yourself; cook with your own hands and feed them. If you continue this for some days, you will find that lots of people will be coming forward to assist you with plenty of money. " — Never, my son, does a doer of good come to grief." (Gita, VI. 40).

Disciple: Yes, it is true. But may not that kind of continuous work become a source of bondage in the long run?

Swamiji: If you have no eye to the fruits of work, and if you have a passionate longing to go beyond all selfish desires, then these good works will help to break your bonds, I tell you. How thoughtless of you to say that such work will lead to bondage! Such disinterested work is the only means of rooting out the bondage due to selfish work. " — There is no other way out" (Shvetâsvatara Upanishad, III. 8).

Disciple: Your words encourage me to hear in detail about your ideas of the Feeding Home and Home of Service.

Swamiji: We must build small well-ventilated rooms for the poor. Only two or three of them will live in each room. They must be given good bedding, clean clothes, and so on. There will be a doctor for them, who will inspect them once or twice a week according to his convenience. The Sevâshrama (Home of Service) will be as a ward attached to the Annasatra, where the sick will be nursed. Then, gradually, as funds will accumulate, we shall build a big kitchen. The Annasatra must be astir with constant shouts of food demanded and supplied. The rice-gruel must run into the Ganga and whiten its water! When I see such a Feeding Home started, it will bring solace to my heart.

Disciple: When you have this kind of desire, most likely it will materialise into action in course of time.

Hearing the disciple's words, Swamiji remained motionless for a while, gazing on the Ganga. Then with a beaming countenance he addressed the disciple, saying: "Who knows which of you will have the lion roused up in him, and when? If in a single one amongst you Mother rouses the fire, there will be hundreds of Feeding Homes like that. Knowledge and Power and Devotion — everything exists in the fullest measure in all beings. We only notice the varying degrees of their manifestation and call one great and another little. In the minds of all creatures a screen intervenes as it were and hides the perfect manifestation from view. The moment that is removed, everything is settled; whatever you want, whatever you will desire, will come to pass."

Swamiji continued: "If the Lord wills, we shall make this Math a great centre of harmony. Our Lord is the visible embodiment of the harmony of all ideals. He will be established on earth if we keep alive that spirit of harmony here. We must see to it that people of all creeds and sects, from the Brâhmana down to the Chandâla, may come here and find their respective ideals manifested. The other day when I installed Shri Ramakrishna on the Math grounds, I felt as if his ideas shot forth from this place and flooded the whole universe, sentient and insentient. I, for one, am doing my best, and shall continue to do so — all of you too explain to people the liberal ideas of Shri Ramakrishna; what is the use of merely reading the Vedanta? We must prove the truth of pure Advaitism in practical life. Shankara left this Advaita philosophy in the hills and forests, while I have come to bring it out of those places and scatter it broadcast before the workaday world and society. The lion-roar of Advaita must resound in every hearth and home, in meadows and groves, over hills and plains. Come all of you to my assistance and set yourselves to work."

Disciple: Sir, it appeals to me rather to realise that state through meditation than to manifest it in action.

Swamiji: That is but a state of stupefaction, as under liquor. What will be the use of merely remaining like that? Through the urge of Advaitic realisation, you should sometimes dance wildly and sometimes remain lost to outward sense. Does one feel happy to taste of a good thing by oneself? One should share it with others. Granted that you attain personal liberation by means of the realisation of the Advaita, but what matters it to the world? You must liberate the whole universe before you leave this body. Then only you will be established in the eternal Truth. Has that bliss any match, my boy? You will be established in that bliss of the Infinite which is limitless like the skies. You will be struck dumb to find your presence everywhere in the world of soul and matter. You will feel the whole sentient and insentient world as your own self. Then you can't help treating all with the same kindness as you show towards yourself. This is indeed practical Vedanta. Do you understand me? Brahman is one, but is at the same time appearing to us as many, on the relative plane. Name and form are at the root of this relativity. For instance, what do you find when you abstract name and form from a jar? Only earth, which is its essence. Similarly, through delusion you are thinking of and seeing a jar, a cloth, a monastery, and so on. The phenomenal world depends on this nescience which obstructs knowledge and which has no real existence. One sees variety such as wife, children, body, mind — only in the world created by nescience by means of name and form. As soon as this nescience is removed, the realisation of Brahman which eternally exists is the result.

Disciple: Where has the nescience come from?

Swamiji: Where it has come from I shall tell you later on. When you began to run, mistaking the rope for the snake, did the rope actually turn into a snake? Or was it not your ignorance which put you to flight in that way?

Disciple: I did it from sheer ignorance.

Swamiji: Well, then, consider whether, when you will again come to know the rope as rope, you will not laugh at your previous ignorance. Will not name and form appear to be a delusion then?

Disciple: They will.

Swamiji: If that be so, the name and form turn out to be unreal. Thus Brahman, the Eternal Existence, proves to be the only reality. Only through this twilight of nescience you think this is your wife, that is your child, this is your own, that is not your own, and so on, and fail to realise the existence of the Atman, the illuminator of everything. When through the Guru's instructions and your own conviction you will see, not this world of name and form, but the essence which lies as its substratum then only you will realise your identity with the whole universe from the Creator down to a clump of grass, then only you will get the state in which " — The knots of the heart are cut asunder and all doubts are dispelled".

Disciple: Sir, one wishes to know of the origin and cessation of this nescience.

Swamiji: You have understood, I presume, that a thing that ceases to exist afterwards is a phenomenon merely? He who has truly realised Brahman will say — where is nescience, in faith? He sees the rope as rope only, and never as the snake. And he laughs at the alarm of those who see it as the snake. For this reason, nescience has no absolute reality. You can call nescience neither real nor unreal; "सन्नाप्यसन्नाप्युभयात्मिका नो — Neither real, nor unreal, nor a mixture of both". About a thing that is thus proved to be false, neither question nor answer is of any significance. Moreover, any question on such a thing is unreasonable. I shall explain how. Are not this question and answer made from the standpoint of name and form, of time and space? And can you explain Brahman which transcends time and space, by means of questions and answers? Hence the Shastras and Mantras and such other things are only relatively, and not absolutely, true. Nescience has verily no essence to call its own; how then can you understand it? When Brahman will manifest Itself, there will be no more room for such questions. Have you not heard that story of Shri Ramakrishna about the shoemaker coolie? The moment one recognises nescience, it vanishes.

Disciple: But, sir, whence has this nescience come?

Swamiji: How can that come which has no existence at all? It must exist first, to admit the possibility of coming.

Disciple: How then did this world of souls and matter originate?

Swamiji: There is only one Existence — Brahman. You are but seeing That under different forms and names, through the veil of name and form which are unreal.

Disciple: But why this unreal name and form? Whence have they come?

Swamiji: The Shastras have described this ingrained notion or ignorance as almost endless in a series. But it has a termination, while Brahman ever remains as It is, without suffering the least change, like the rope which causes the delusion of the snake. Therefore the conclusion of the Vedanta is that the whole universe has been superimposed on Brahman — appearing like a juggler's trick. It has not caused the least aberration of Brahman from Its real nature. Do you understand me?

Disciple: One thing I cannot yet understand.

Swamiji: What is that?

Disciple: You have just said that creation, maintenance, and dissolution, etc. are superimposed on Brahman, and have no absolute existence. But how can that be? One can never have the delusion of something that one has not already experienced. Just as one who has never seen a snake cannot mistake a rope for a snake, so how can one who has not experienced this creation, come to mistake Brahman for the creation? Therefore creation must have been, or is, to have given rise to the delusion of creation. But this brings in a dualistic position.

Swamiji: The man of realisation will in the first place refute your objection by stating that to his vision creation and things of that sort do not at all appear. He sees Brahman and Brahman alone. He sees the rope and not the snake. If you argue that you, at any rate, are seeing this creation, or snake – then he will try to bring home to you the real nature of the rope, with a view to curing your defective vision. When through his instructions and your reasoning you will be able to realise the truth of the rope, or Brahman, then this delusive idea of the snake, or creation, will vanish. At that time, what else can you call this delusive idea of creation, maintenance, and dissolution, but a superimposition on the Brahman? If this appearance of creation etc. has continued as a beginningless series, let it do so; no advantage will be gained by settling this question. Until Brahman is realised as vividly as a fruit on the palm of one's hand this question cannot be adequately settled, and then neither such a question crops up, nor is there need for a solution. The tasting of the reality of Brahman is then like a dumb man tasting something nice, but without the power to express his feelings.

Disciple: What then will be the use of reasoning about it so much?

Swamiji: Reasoning is necessary to understand the point intellectually. But the Reality transcends reasoning: "नैषा तर्केण मतिरापनेया – This conviction cannot be reached through reasoning."

In the course of such conversation Swamiji reached the Math, accompanied by the disciple. Swamiji then explained to the Sannyasins and Brahmacharins of the Math the gist of the above discussion on Brahman. While going upstairs, he remarked to the disciple, "नायमात्मा बलहीनेन लभ्यः – This Atman cannot be attained by the weak."

X

(From the Diary of a Disciple (Shri Sharat Chandra Chakravarty, B.A.))

(Translated from Bengali)

[Place: The rented Math premises at Belur. Year: 1899.]

The Bengali fortnightly magazine, *Udbodhan*, was just started by Swami Trigunatita under the direction of Swamiji for spreading the religious views of Shri Ramakrishna among the general public. After the first number came out the disciple came to the Math at Nilambar Babu's garden one day. Swamiji started the following conversation with him about the *Udbodhan*.

Swamiji: (Humorously caricaturing the name of the magazine) Have you seen the *Udbandhana*? (The word means "suicide by hanging".)

Disciple: Yes, sir; it is a good number.

Swamiji: We must mould the ideas, language, and everything of this magazine in a new fashion.

Disciple: How?

Swamiji: Not only must we give out Shri Ramakrishna's ideas to all, but we must also introduce a new vigour into the Bengali language. For instance, the frequent use of verbs diminishes the force of a language. We must restrict the use of verbs by the use of adjectives. Begin to write articles in that way, and show them to me before you give them to print in the Udbodhan.

Disciple: Sir, it is impossible for any other man to labour for this magazine in the way Swami Trigunatita does.

Swamiji: Do you think these Sannyasin children of Shri Ramakrishna are born simply to sit under trees lighting Dhuni-fires? Whenever any of them will take up some work, people will be astonished to see their energy. Learn from them how to work. Here, for instance, Trigunatita has given up his spiritual practices, his meditation and everything, to carry out my orders, and has set himself to work. Is this a matter of small sacrifice? What an amount of love for me is at the back of this spirit of work, do you see? He will not stop short of success! Have you householders such determination?

Disciple: But, sir, it looks rather odd in our eyes that Sannyasins in ochre robe should go about from door to door as the Swami is doing.

Swamiji: Why? The circulation of the magazine is only for the good of the householders. By the spread of new ideas within the country the public at large will be benefited. Do you think this unselfish work is any way inferior to devotional practices? Our object is to do good to humanity. We have no idea of making money from the income of this paper. We have renounced everything and have no wives or children to provide for after our death. If the paper be a success, the whole of its income will be spent in the service of humanity. Its surplus money will be profitably spent in the opening of monasteries and homes of service in different places and all sorts of work of public utility. We are not certainly working like householders with the plan of filling our own pockets. Know for certain that all our movements are for the good of others.

Disciple: Even then, all will not be able to appreciate this spirit.

Swamiji: What if they cannot? It neither adds nor takes away anything from us. We do not take up any work with an eye to criticism.

Disciple: So this magazine will be a fortnightly. We should like it to be a weekly.

Swamiji: Yes, but where are the funds? If through the grace of Shri Ramakrishna funds are raised, it can be made into a daily even, in future. A hundred thousand copies may be struck off daily and distributed free in every street and lane of Calcutta.

Disciple: This idea of yours is a capital one.

Swamiji: I have a mind to make the paper self-supporting first, and then set you up as its editor. You have not yet got the capacity to make any enterprise stand on its legs. That is reserved only for these all-renouncing Sannyasins to do. They will work themselves to death, but never yield. Whereas a little resistance or just a trifle of criticism is bewildering to you.

Disciple: Sir, the other day I saw that Swami Trigunatita worshipped the photograph of Sri Ramakrishna in the Press before opening the work and asked for your blessings for the success of the work.

Swamiji: Well, Shri Ramakrishna is our centre. Each one of us is a ray of that light-centre. So Trigunatita worshipped Shri Ramakrishna before beginning the work, did he? It was excellently done. But he told me nothing of it.

Disciple: Sir, he fears you and yesterday he told me to come to you and ask your opinion of the first issue of the magazine, after which, he said, he would see you.

Swamiji: Tell him when you go that I am exceedingly delighted with his work. Give him my loving blessings. And all of you help him as far as you can. You will be doing Shri Ramakrishna's work by that.

Immediately after saying these words Swamiji called Swami Brahmananda to him and directed him to give Swami Trigunatita more money for the *Udbodhan* if it was needed.

The same evening, after supper, Swamiji again referred to the topic of *Udbodhan* in the following words:

"In the *Udbodhan* we must give the public only positive ideas. Negative thoughts weaken men. Do you not find that where parents are constantly taxing their sons to read and write, telling them they will never learn anything, and calling them fools and so forth, the latter do actually turn out to be so in many cases? If you speak kind words to boys and encourage them, they are bound to improve in time. What holds good of children, also holds good of children in the region of higher thoughts. If you can give them positive ideas, people will grow up to be men and learn to stand on their own legs. In language and literature, in poetry and the arts, in everything we must point out not the mistakes that people are making in their thoughts and actions, but the way in which they will gradually be able to do these things better. Pointing out mistakes wounds a man's feelings. We have seen how Shri Ramakrishna would encourage even those whom we considered as worthless and change the very course of their lives thereby! His very method of teaching was a unique phenomenon."

After a short pause, Swamiji continued, "Never take the preaching of religion to mean the turning up of one's nose at everything and at everybody. In matters physical, mental, and spiritual – in everything we must give men positive ideas and never hate anybody. It is your hatred of one another that has brought about your degradation. Now we shall have to raise men by scattering broadcast only positive thoughts. First we must raise the whole Hindu race in this way and then the whole world. That is why Shri Ramakrishna incarnated. He never destroyed a single man's special inclinations. He gave words of hope and encouragement even to the most degraded of persons and lifted them up. We too must follow in his footsteps and lift all up, and rouse them. Do you understand?

"Your history, literature, mythology, and all other Shastras are simply frightening people. They are only telling them, 'You will go to hell, you are doomed!' Therefore has this lethargy crept into the very vitals of India. Hence we must explain to men in simple words the highest ideas of the Vedas and the Vedanta. Through the imparting of moral principles, good behaviour, and education we must make the Chandâla come up to the level of the Brahmana. Come, write out all these things in the *Udbodhan* and awaken everyone, young and old, man and woman. Then only shall I know that your study of the Vedas and Vedanta has been a success. What do you say? Will you be able to do this?"

Disciple: Through your blessings and command I think I shall succeed in everything.

Swamiji: Another thing. You must learn to make the physique very strong and teach the same to others. Don't you find me exercising every day with dumb-bells even now? Walk in the morning and evenings and do physical labour. Body and mind must run parallel. It won't do to depend on others in everything. When the necessity of strengthening the physique is brought home to people, they will exert themselves of their own accord. It is to make them feel this need that education is necessary at the present moment.

XI

(From the Diary of a Disciple (Shri Sharat Chandra Chakravarty, B.A.))

(Translated from Bengali)

[Place: The Belur Math (under construction). Year: 1899.]

Disciple: Why is it, Swamiji, that our society and country have come to such degradation?

Swamiji: It is you who are responsible for it.

Disciple: How, sir? You surprise me.

Swamiji: You have been despising the lower classes of the country for a very long time and, as a result, you have now become the objects of contempt in the eyes of the world.

Disciple: When did you find us despising them?

Swamiji: Why, you priest-class never let the non-Brahmin class read the Vedas and Vedanta and all such weighty Shastras — never touch them even. You have only kept them down. It is you who have always done like that through selfishness. It was the Brahmins who made a monopoly of the religious books and kept the question of sanction and prohibition in their own hands. And repeatedly calling the other races of India low and vile, they put this belief into their heads that they were really such. If you tell a man, "You are low, you are vile", in season and out of season, then he is bound to believe in course of time that he is really such. This is called hypnotism. The non-Brahmin classes are now slowly rousing themselves. Their faith in Brahminical scriptures and Mantras is getting shaken. Through the spread of Western education all the tricks of the Brahmins are giving way, like the banks of the Padmâ in the rainy season. Do you not see that?

Disciple: Yes, sir, the stricture of orthodoxy is gradually lessening nowadays.

Swamiji: It is as it should be. The Brahmins, in fact, gradually took a course of gross immorality and oppression. Through selfishness they introduced a large number of strange, non-Vedic, immoral, and unreasonable doctrines – simply to keep intact their own prestige. And the fruits of that they are reaping forthwith.

Disciple: What may these fruits be, sir?

Swamiji: Don't you perceive them? It is simply due to your having despised the masses of India that you have now been living a life of slavery for the last thousand years; it is therefore that you are the objects of hatred in the eyes of foreigners and are looked upon with indifference by your countrymen.

Disciple: But, sir, even now it is the Brahmins who direct all ceremonials, and people are observing them according to the opinions of the Brahmins. Why then do you speak like that?

Swamiji: I don't find it. Where do the tenfold Samskâras or purifying ceremonies enjoined by the Shastras obtain still? Well, I have travelled the whole of India, and everywhere I have found society to be guided by local usages which are condemned by the Shrutis and Smritis. Popular customs, local usages, and observances prevalent among women only – have not these taken the place of the Smritis everywhere? Who obeys, and whom? If you can but spend enough money, the priest-class is ready to write out whatever sanctions or prohibitions you want! How many of them read the Vedic Kalpa (Ritual), Grihya and Shrauta Sutras? Then, look, here in Bengal the code of Raghunandana is obeyed; a little farther on you will find the code of Mitâkshâra in vogue; while in another part the code of Manu holds sway! You seem to think that the same laws hold good everywhere! What I want therefore is to introduce the study of the Vedas by stimulating a greater regard for them in the minds of the people, and to pass everywhere the injunctions of the Vedas.

Disciple: Sir, is it possible nowadays to set them going?

Swamiji: It is true that all the ancient Vedic laws will not have a go, but if we introduce additions and alterations in them to suit the needs of the times, codify them, and hold them up as a new model to society, why will they not pass current?

Disciple: Sir, I was under the impression that at least the injunctions of Manu were being obeyed all over India even now.

Swamiji: Nothing of the kind. Just look to your own province and see how the Vâmâchâra (immoral practices) of the Tantras has entered into your very marrow. Even modern Vaishnavism, which is the skeleton of the defunct Buddhism, is saturated with Vamachara! We must stem the tide of this Vamachara, which is contrary to the spirit of the Vedas.

Disciple: Sir, is it possible now to cleanse this Aegean stable?

Swamiji: What nonsense do you say, you coward! You have well-nigh thrown the country into ruin by crying, 'It is impossible, it is impossible!' What cannot human effort achieve?

Disciple: But, sir, such a state of things seems impossible unless sages like Manu and Yâjnavalkya are again born in the country.

Swamiji: Goodness gracious! Was it not purity and unselfish labour that made them Manu and Yajnavalkya, or was it something else? Well, we ourselves can be far greater than even Manu and Yajnavalkya if we try to; why will not our views prevail then?

Disciple: Sir, it is you who said just now that we must revive the ancient usages and observances within the country. How then can we think lightly of sages like Manu and the rest?

Swamiji: What an absurd deduction! You altogether miss my point. I have only said that the ancient Vedic customs must be remodelled according to the need of the society and the times, and passed under a new form in the land. Have I not?

Disciple: Yes, sir.

Swamiji: What, then, were you talking? You have read the Shastras, and my hope and faith rest in men like you. Understand my words in their true spirit, and apply yourselves to work in their light.

Disciple: But, sir, who will listen to us? Why should our countrymen accept them?

Swamiji: If you can truly convince them and practise what you preach, they must. If, on the contrary, like a coward you simply utter Shlokas as a parrot, be a mere talker and quote authority only, without showing them in action — then who will care to listen to you?

Disciple: Please give me some advice in brief about social reform.

Swamiji: Why, I have given you advice enough; now put at least something in practice. Let the world see that your reading of the scriptures and listening to me has been a success. The codes of Manu and lots of other books that you have read – what is their basis and underlying purpose? Keeping that basis intact, compile in the manner of the ancient Rishis the essential truths of them and supplement them with thoughts that are suited to the times; only take care that all races and all sects throughout India be really benefited by following these rules. Just write out a Smriti like that; I shall revise it.

Disciple: Sir, it is not an easy task; and even if such a Smriti be written, will it be accepted?

Swamiji: Why not? Just write it out. "कालो ह्ययं निरवधिर्विपुला च पृथ्वी – Time is infinite, and the world is vast." If you write it in the proper way, there must come a day when it will be accepted. Have faith in yourself. You people were once the Vedic Rishis. Only, you have come in different forms, that's all. I see it clear as daylight that you all have infinite power in you. Rouse that up; arise, arise – apply yourselves heart and soul, gird up your loins. What will you do with wealth and fame that are so transitory? Do you know what I think? I don't care for Mukti and all that. My mission is to arouse within you all such ideas; I am ready to undergo a hundred thousand rebirths to train up a single man.

Disciple: But, sir, what will be the use of undertaking such works? Is not death stalking behind?

Swamiji: Fie upon you! If you die, you will die but once. Why will you die every minute of your life by constantly harping on death like a coward?

Disciple: All right, sir, I may not think of death, but what good will come of any kind of work in this evanescent world?

Swamiji: My boy, when death is inevitable, is it not better to die like heroes than as stocks and stones? And what is the use of living a day or two more in this transitory world? It is better to wear out than to rust out – specially for the sake of doing the least good to others.

Disciple: It is true, sir. I beg pardon for troubling you so much.

Swamiji: I don't feel tired even if I talk for two whole nights to an earnest inquirer; I can give up food and sleep and talk and talk. Well, if

I have a mind, I can sit up in Samadhi in a Himalayan cave. And you see that nowadays through the Mother's grace I have not to think about food, it comes anyhow. Why then don't I do so? And why am I here? Only the sight of the country's misery and the thought of its future do not let me remain quiet any more! – Even Samadhi and all that appear as futile – even the sphere of Brahmâ with its enjoyments becomes insipid! My vow of life is to think of your welfare. The day that vow will be fulfilled, I shall leave this body and make a straight run up!

Hearing Swamiji's words the disciple sat speechless for a while, gazing at him, wondering in his heart. Then, with a view to taking his leave, he saluted Swamiji reverently and asked his permission to go.

Swamiji: Why do you want to go? Why not live in the Math? Your mind will again be polluted if you go back to the worldly-minded. See here, how fresh is the air, there is the Ganga, and the Sadhus (holy men) are practising meditation, and holding lofty talks! While the moment you will go to Calcutta, you will be thinking of nasty stuff.

The disciple joyfully replied, "All right, sir, I shall stay today at the Math."

Swamiji: Why "today"? Can't you live here for good? What is the use of going back to the world?

The disciple bent down his head, hearing Swamiji's words. Various thoughts crowded into his brain and kept him speechless.

XII

(From the Diary of a Disciple (Shri Sharat Chandra Chakravarty, B.A.))

(Translated from Bengali)

[Place: The Belur Math (under construction). Year: beginning of 1899.]

Today Swamiji is walking round the new Math grounds in the afternoon in company with the disciple. Standing at a little distance off the Bael tree Swamiji took to singing slowly a Bengali song: (This is one of the songs sung in the homes of Bengal on the eve of Durgâ Pujâ.) "O Himalaya, Ganesh is auspicious to me" etc., ending with the line – "And many Dandis (Sannyasins) and Yogis with matted hair will also come." While singing the song Swamiji repeated this line to the disciple and said, "Do you understand? In course of time many Sadhus and Sannyasins will come here." Saying this he sat under the tree and remarked, "The ground under the Bilva tree is very holy. Meditating here quickly brings about an awakening of the religious instinct. Shri Ramakrishna used to say so."

Disciple: Sir, those who are devoted to the discrimination between the Self and not-Self – have they any need to consider the auspiciousness of place, time, and so forth?

Swamiji: Those who are established in the knowledge of the Atman have no need for such discrimination, but that state is not attained off-hand. It comes as the result of long practice. Therefore in the beginning one has to take the help of external aids and learn to stand on one's own legs. Later on, when one is established in the knowledge of the Atman, there is no more need for any external aid.

The various methods of spiritual practice that have been laid down in the scriptures are all for the attainment of the knowledge of the Atman. Of course these practices vary according to the qualifications of different aspirants. But they also are a kind of work, and so long as there is work, the Atman is not discovered. The obstacles to the manifestation of the Atman are overcome by practices as laid down in the scriptures; but work has no power of directly manifesting the Atman, it is only effective in removing some veils that cover knowledge. Then the Atman manifests by Its own effulgence. Do you see? Therefore does your commentator (Shankara) say, "In our knowledge of Brahman, there cannot be the least touch of work."

Disciple: But, sir, since the obstacles to Self-manifestation are not overcome without the performance of work in some form or other, therefore indirectly work stands as a means to knowledge.

Swamiji: From the standpoint of the causal chain, it so appears *prima facie*. Taking up this view it is stated in the Purva-Mimâmsâ that work for a definite end infallibly produces a definite result. But the vision of the Atman which is Absolute is not to be compassed by means of work. For the rule with regard to a seeker of the Atman is that he should undergo spiritual practice, but have no eye to its results. It follows thence that these practices are simply the cause of the purification of the aspirant's mind. For if the Atman could be directly realised as a result of these practices, then scriptures would not have enjoined on the aspirant to give up the results of work. So it is with a view to combating the Purva-Mimamsa doctrine of work with motive producing results, that the philosophy of work without motive has been set forth in the Gita. Do you see?

Disciple: But, sir, if one has to renounce the fruits of work, why should one be induced to undertake work which is always troublesome?

Swamiji: In this human life, one cannot help doing some kind of work always. When man has perforce to do some work, Karma-Yoga enjoins on him to do it in such a way as will bring freedom through the realisation of the Atman. As to your objection that none will be induced to work — the answer is, that whatever work you do has some motive behind it; but when by the long performance of work, one notices that one work merely leads to another, through a round of births and rebirths, then the awakened discrimination of man naturally begins to question itself, "Where is the end to this interminable chain of work?" It is then that he appreciates the full import of the words of the Lord in the Gita: "Inscrutable is the course of work. "Therefore when the aspirant finds that work with motive brings no happiness, then he renounces action. But man is so constituted that to him the performance of work is a necessity, so what work should he take up? He takes up some unselfish work, but gives up all desire for its fruits. For he has known then that in those fruits of work lie countless seeds of future births and deaths. Therefore the knower of Brahman renounces all actions. Although to outward appearances he engages himself in some work, he has no attachment to it. Such men have been described in the scriptures as Karma-Yogins.

Disciple: Is then the work without motive of the unselfish knower of Brahman like the activities of a lunatic?

Swamiji: Why so? Giving up the fruits of work means not to perform work for the good of one's own body or mind. The knower of Brahman never seeks his own happiness. But what is there to prevent him from doing work for the welfare of others? Whatever work he does without attachment for its fruits brings only good to the world – it is all "for the good of the many, for the happiness of the many". Shri Ramakrishna used to say, "They never take a false step". Haven't you read in the *Uttara-Râma-Charita*, " ऋषीणाम् पुनराद्यानां वाचमर्थोऽनुधावति – The words of the ancient Rishis have always some meaning, they are never false?" When the mind is merged in the Atman by the suppression of all modifications, it produces "a dispassion for the enjoyment of fruits of work here or hereafter"; there remains no desire in the mind for any enjoyment here, or, after death, in any heavenly sphere. There is no action and interaction of desires in the mind. But when the mind descends from the superconscious state into the world of "I and mine", then by the momentum of previous work or habit, or Samskaras (impressions), the functions of the body go on as before. The mind then is generally in the superconscious state; eating and other functions of the body are done from mere necessity, and the body-consciousness is very much attenuated. Whatever work is done after reaching this transcendental state is done rightly; it conduces to the real well-being of men and the world; for then the mind of the doer is not contaminated by selfishness or calculation of personal gain or loss. The Lord has created this wonderful universe, remaining always in the realm of superconsciousness; therefore there is nothing imperfect in this world. So I was saying that the actions which the knower of the Atman does without attachment for fruits are never imperfect, but they conduce to the real well-being of men and the world.

Disciple: Sir, you said just now that knowledge and work are contradictory, that in the supreme knowledge there is no room at all for work, or in other words, that by means of work the realisation of Brahman cannot be attained. Why then do you now and then speak words calculated to awaken great Rajas (activity)? You were telling me the other day, "Work, work, work – there is no other way."

Swamiji: Going round the whole world, I find that people of this country are immersed in great Tamas (inactivity), compared with people of other countries. On the outside, there is a simulation of the Sâttvika (calm and balanced) state, but inside, downright inertness like that of stocks and stones – what work will be done in the world by such people? How long can such an inactive, lazy, and sensual people live in the world? First travel in Western countries, then contradict my words. How much of enterprise and devotion to work, how much enthusiasm and manifestation of Rajas are there in the lives of the Western people! While, in your own country, it is as if the blood has become congealed in the heart, so that it cannot circulate in the veins — as if paralysis has overtaken the body and it has become languid. So my idea is first to make the people active by developing their Rajas, and thus make them fit for the struggle for existence. With no strength in the body, no enthusiasm at heart, and no originality in the brain, what will they do — these lumps of dead matter! By stimulating them I want to bring life into them — to this I have dedicated my life. I will rouse them through the infallible power of Vedic Mantras. I am born to proclaim to them that fearless message — "Arise! Awake!" Be you my helpers in this work! Go from village to village, from one portion of the country to another, and preach this message of fearlessness to all, from the Brahmin to the Chandâla. Tell each and all that infinite power resides within them, that they are sharers of immortal Bliss. Thus rouse up the Rajas within them — make them fit for the struggle for existence, and then speak to them about salvation. First make the people of the country stand on their legs by rousing their inner power, first let them learn to have good food and clothes and plenty of enjoyment — then tell them how to be free from this bondage of enjoyment.

Laziness, meanness, and hypocrisy have covered the whole length and breadth of the country. Can an intelligent man look on all this and remain quiet? Does it not bring tears to the eyes? Madras, Bombay, Punjab, Bengal — whichever way I look, I see no signs of life. You are thinking yourselves highly educated. What nonsense have you learnt? Getting by heart the thoughts of others in a foreign language, and stuffing your brain with them and taking some university degrees, you consider yourselves educated! Fie upon you! Is this education? What is the goal of your education? Either a clerkship, or being a roguish lawyer, or at the most a Deputy Magistracy, which is another form of clerkship — isn't that all? Open your eyes and see what a piteous cry for food is rising in the land of Bharata, proverbial for its wealth! Will your education fulfil this want? Never. With the help of Western science set yourselves to dig the earth and produce food-stuffs — not by means of mean servitude of others — but by discovering new avenues to production, by your own exertions aided by Western science. Therefore I teach the people of this country to be full of activities, so as to be able to produce food and clothing for themselves. For want of food and clothing and plunged in anxiety for it, the country has come to ruin — what are you doing to remedy this? Throw aside your scriptures in the Ganga and teach the people first the means of procuring their food and clothing, and then you will find time to read to them the scriptures. If their material wants are not removed by the rousing of intense activity, none will listen to words of spirituality. Therefore I say, first rouse the inherent power of the Atman within you, then, rousing the faith of the general people in that power as much as you can, teach them first of all to make provision for food, and then teach them religion. There is no time to sit idle — who knows when death will overtake one?

While saying these words, a mingled expression of remorse, sorrow, compassion, and power shone on his face. Looking at his majestic appearance, the disciple was awed into silence. A little while afterwards Swamiji said again, "That activity and self-reliance must come in the people of the country in time — I see it clearly. There is no escape. The intelligent man can distinctly see the vision of the next three Yugas (ages) ahead. Ever since the advent of Shri Ramakrishna the eastern horizon has been aglow with the dawning rays of the sun which in course of time will illumine the country with the splendour of the midday sun."

XIII

(From the Diary of a Disciple (Shri Sharat Chandra Chakravarty, B.A.))

(Translated from Bengali)

[Place: The Belur Math. Beginning of 1899.]

The present Math buildings are almost complete now. Swamiji is not in good health; therefore doctors have advised him to go out on a boat in the mornings and evenings on the Ganga.

Today is Sunday. The disciple is sitting in Swamiji's room and conversing with him. About this time Swamiji framed certain rules for the guidance of the Sannyasins and Brahmacharins of the Math, the object of which was to keep them from indiscriminate mixing with worldly people. The conversation turned on this topic.

Swamiji: Nowadays I feel a peculiar smell of lax self-control in the dress and clothes of worldly people; therefore I have made it a rule in the Math that householders should not sit or lie on the beds of Sadhus. Formerly I used to read in the Shastras that such a smell is felt, and therefore Sannyasins cannot bear the smell of householders. Now I see it is true. By strictly observing the rules that have been framed, the Brahmacharins will in time grow into genuine Sannyasins. When they are established in the ideal of Sannyasa, they will be able to mix on an equal footing with worldly men without any harm. But now if they are not kept within the barriers of strict rules, they will all go wrong. In order to attain to ideal Brahmacharya one has in the beginning to observe strict rules regarding chastity. Not only should one keep oneself strictly aloof from the least association with the opposite sex, but also give up the company of married people even.

The disciple who was a householder was awed at these words of Swamiji, felt dejected that he would not be able to associate freely as before with the Sadhus of the Math and said, "Sir, I feel more intimacy with the Math and its inmates than with my own family. As if they are known to me from a long long time. The unbounded freedom that I enjoy in the Math, I feel nowhere else in the world."

Swamiji: All those who are pure in spirit will feel like that here. Those who do not feel so must be taken as not belonging to this Math and its ideals. That is the reason why many people come here out of mere sensation-mongering and then run away. Those who are devoid of continence and are running after money day and night will never be able to appreciate the ideals of the Math, nor regard the Math people as their own. The Sannyasins of this Math are not like those of old, ash-besmeared, with matted hair and iron tongs in their hands, and curing disease by medicinal titbits; therefore seeing the contrast, people cannot appreciate them. The ways, movements and ideas of our Master were all cast in a new mould, so we are also of a new type. Sometimes dressed like gentlemen, we are engaged in lecturing; at other times, throwing all aside, with " Hara, Hara, Vyom Vyom " on the lips, ash-clad, we are immersed in meditation and austerities in mountains and forests.

Now it won't do to merely quote the authority of our ancient books. The tidal wave of Western civilisation is now rushing over the length and breadth of the country. It won't do now simply to sit in meditation on mountain tops without realising in the least its usefulness. Now is wanted – as said in the Gita by the Lord – intense Karma-Yoga, with unbounded courage and indomitable strength in the heart. Then only will the people of the country be roused, otherwise they will continue to be as much in the dark as you are.

The day is nearly ended. Swamiji came downstairs, dressed for the boating excursion on the Ganga. Swamiji, accompanied by the disciple and two others, boarded the boat, which passed the Dakshineswar temple and reached Panihati where it was anchored below the garden-house of Babu Govinda Kumar Chaudhury. It has once been proposed to rent this house for the use of the Math. Swamiji descended from the boat, went round the house and the garden and looking over the place minutely said, "The garden is nice but is at a great distance from Calcutta. The devotees of Shri Ramakrishna would have been put to trouble to walk such a long distance from Calcutta. It is fortunate that the Math has not been established here." The boat then returned to the Math amid the enveloping darkness.

XIV

(From the Diary of a Disciple (Shri Sharat Chandra Chakravarty, B.A.))

(Translated from Bengali)

[Place: Belur Math. Beginning of 1899.]

The disciple has today come to the Math with Nag Mahashaya in company.

Swamiji to Nag Mahashaya (saluting him): You are all right, I hope?

Nag Mahashaya: I have come today to visit you. Glory to Shankara! Glory to Shankara! I am blessed today verily with the sight of Shiva!

Saying these words, Nag Mahashaya out of reverence stood with joined hands before him.

Swamiji: How is your health?

Nag Mahashaya: Why are you asking about this trifling body — this cage of flesh and bones? Verily I am blessed today to see you.

Saying these words, Nag Mahashaya prostrated before Swamiji.

Swamiji (lifting him up): Why are you doing that to me?

Nag Mahashaya: I see with my inner eye that today I am blessed with the vision of Shiva Himself. Glory to Ramakrishna!

Swamiji (addressing the disciple): Do you see? How real Bhakti transforms human nature! Nag Mahashaya has lost himself in the Divine, his body-consciousness has vanished altogether. (To Swami Premananda) Get some Prasada for Nag Mahashaya.

Nag Mahashaya: Prasada! (To Swamiji with folded hands) Seeing you, all my earthly hunger has vanished today.

The Brahmacharins and Sannyasins of the Math were studying the Upanishads. Swamiji said to them, "Today a great devotee of Shri Ramakrishna has come amongst us. Let it be a holiday in honour of Nag Mahashaya's visit to the Math." So all closed their books and sat in a circle round Nag Mahashaya; Swamiji also sat in front of him.

Swamiji (addressing all): Do you see? Look at Nag Mahashaya; he is a householder, yet he has no knowledge of the mundane existence; he always lives lost in Divine consciousness. (To Nag Mahashaya) Please tell us and these Brahmacharins something about Shri Ramakrishna.

Nag Mahashaya (in reverence): What do you say, sir? What shall I say? I have come to see you – the hero, the helper in the divine play of Shri Ramakrishna. Now will people appreciate his message and teachings. Glory to Ramakrishna!

Swamiji: It is you who have really appreciated and understood Shri Ramakrishna. We are only spent in useless wanderings.

Nag Mahashaya: What do you say, sir? You are the image of Shri Ramakrishna – the obverse and reverse of the same coin. Those who have eyes, let them see.

Swamiji: Is the starting of these Maths and Ashramas etc. a step in the right direction?

Nag Mahashaya: I am an insignificant being, what do I understand? Whatever you do, I know for a certainty, will conduce to the well-being of the world – ay, of the world.

Many out of reverence proceeded to take the dust of Nag Mahashaya's feet, which made him much agitated. Swamiji, addressing all, said, "Don't act so as to cause pain to Nag Mahashaya; he feels uncomfortable." Hearing this everybody desisted.

Swamiji: Do please come and stay at the Math. You will be an object-lesson to the boys here.

Nag Mahashaya: I once asked Shri Ramakrishna about that, to which he replied, "Stay as a householder as you are doing." Therefore I am continuing in that life. I see you all occasionally and feel myself blessed.

Swamiji: I will go to your place once.

Nag Mahashaya, mad with joy, said, "Shall such a day dawn? My place will be made holy by your visit, like Varanasi. Shall I be so fortunate as that!"

Swamiji: Well, I have the desire. Now it depends on "Mother" to take me there.

Nag Mahashaya: Who will understand you? Unless the inner vision opens, nobody can understand you. Only Shri Ramakrishna understood you; all else have simply put faith in his words, but none has understood you really.

Swamiji: Now my one desire is to rouse the country – the sleeping leviathan that has lost all faith in his power and makes no response. If I can wake it up to a sense of the Eternal Religion then I shall know that Shri Ramakrishna's advent and our birth are fruitful. That is the one desire in my heart: Mukti and all else appear of no consequence to me. Please give me your blessings that I may succeed.

Nag Mahashaya: Shri Ramakrishna will bless! who can turn the course of your will? Whatever you will, shall come to pass.

Swamiji: Well, nothing comes to pass without his will behind it.

Nag Mahashaya: Your will and his have become one. Whatever is your will is his. Glory to Shri Ramakrishna!

Swamiji: To work one requires a strong body; since coming to this country, I am not doing well; in the West I was in very good health.

Nag Mahashaya: "Whenever one is born in a body," Shri Ramakrishna used to say, "one has to pay the house tax." Disease and sorrow are the tax. But your body is a box of gold *mohurs*, and very great care should be taken of it. But who will do it? Who will understand? Only Shri Ramakrishna understood. Glory to Ramakrishna!

Swamiji: All at the Math take great care of me.

Nag Mahashaya: It will be to their good if they do it, whether they know it or not. If proper attention is not paid to your body, then the chances are that it will fall off.

Swamiji: Nag Mahashaya, I do not fully understand whether what I am doing is right or not. At particular times I feel a great inclination to work in a certain direction, and I work according to that. Whether it is for good or evil, I cannot understand.

Nag Mahashaya: Well, Shri Ramakrishna said, "The treasure is now locked." — Therefore he does not let you know fully. The moment you know it, your play of human life will be at an end.

Swamiji was pondering something with steadfast gaze. Then Swami Premananda brought some Prasada for Nag Mahashaya who was ecstatic with joy. Shortly after Nag Mahashaya found Swamiji slowly digging the ground with a spade near the pond, and held him by the hand saying, "When we are present, why should you do that?" Swamiji leaving the spade walked about the garden talking the while, and began to narrate to a disciple, "After Shri Ramakrishna's passing away we heard one day that Nag Mahashaya lay fasting in his humbled tiled lodgings in Calcutta. Myself, Swami Turiyananda, and another went together and appeared at Nag Mahashaya's cottage. Seeing us he rose from his bed. We said, 'We shall have our Bhikshâ (food) here today.' At once Nag Mahashaya brought rice, cooking pot, fuel, etc. from the bazaar and began to cook. We thought that we would eat and make Nag Mahashaya also eat. Cooking over, he gave the food to us; we set apart something for him and then sat down to eat. After this, we requested him to take food; he at once broke the pot of rice and striking his forehead began to say: 'Shall I give food to the body in which God has not been realised?' Seeing this we were struck with amazement. Later on after much persuasion we induced him to take some food and then returned."

Swamiji: Will Nag Mahashaya stay in the Math tonight?

Disciple: No, he has some work; he must return today.

Swamiji: Then look for a boat. It is getting dark.

When the boat came, the disciple and Nag Mahashaya saluted Swamiji and started for Calcutta.

XV

(From the Diary of a Disciple (Shri Sharat Chandra Chakravarty, B.A.))

(Translated from Bengali)

[Place: Belur Math. Year: *1899*.]

Swamiji is now in very good health. The disciple has come to the Math on a Sunday morning. After visiting Swamiji he has come downstairs and is discussing the Vedantic scriptures with Swami Nirmalananda. At this moment Swamiji himself came downstairs and addressing the disciple, said, "What were you discussing with Nirmalananda?"

Disciple: Sir, he was saying, "The Brahman of the Vedanta is only known to you and your Swamiji. We on the contrary know that " – Shri Krishna is the Lord Himself. "

Swamiji: What did you say?

Disciple: I said that the Atman is the one Truth, and that Krishna was merely a person who had realised this Atman. Swami Nirmalananda is at heart a believer in the Advaita Vedanta, but outwardly he takes up the dualistic side. His first idea seems to be to moot the personal aspect of the Ishvara and then by a gradual process of reasoning to strengthen the foundations of Vedanta. But as soon as he calls me a "Vaishnava" I forget his real intention and begin a heated discussion with him.

Swamiji: He loves you and so enjoys the fun of teasing you. But why should you be upset by his words? You will also answer, "You, sir, are an atheist, a believer in Nihility."

Disciple: Sir, is there any such statement in the Upanishads that Ishvara is an all-powerful Person? But people generally believe in such an Ishvara.

Swamiji: The highest principle, the Lord of all, cannot be a Person. The Jiva is an individual and the sum total of all Jivas is the Ishvara. In the Jiva, Avidyâ, or nescience, is predominant, but Ishvara controls Maya composed of Avidya and Vidyâ and independently projects this world of moving and immovable things out of Himself. But Brahman transcends both the individual and collective aspects, the Jiva and Ishvara. In Brahman there is no part. It is for the sake of easy comprehension that parts have been imagined in It. That part of Brahman in which there is the superimposition of creation, maintenance and dissolution of the universe has been spoken of as Ishvara in the scriptures, while the other unchangeable portion, with reference to which there is no thought of duality, is indicated as Brahman. But do not on that account think that Brahman is a distinct and separate substance from the Jivas and the universe. The Qualified Monists hold that it is Brahman that has transformed Itself into Jivas and the universe. The Advaitins on the contrary maintain that Jivas and the universe have been merely superimposed on Brahman. But in reality there has been no modification in Brahman. The Advaitin says that the universe consists only of name and form. It endures only so long as there are name and form. When through meditation and other practices name and form are dissolved, then only the transcendent Brahman remains. Then the separate reality of Jivas and the universe is felt no longer. Then it is realised that one is the Eternal Pure Essence of Intelligence, or Brahman. The real nature of the Jiva is Brahman. When the veil of name and form vanishes through meditation etc., then that idea is simply realised. This is the substance of pure Advaita. The Vedas, the Vedanta and all other scriptures only explain this idea in different ways.

Disciple: How then is it true that Ishvara is an almighty Person?

Swamiji: Man is man in so far as he is qualified by the limiting adjunct of mind. Through the mind he has to understand and grasp everything, and therefore whatever he thinks must be limited by the mind. Hence it is the natural tendency of man to argue, from the analogy of his own personality, the personality of Ishvara (God). Man can only think of his ideal as a human being. When buffeted by sorrow in this world of disease and death he is driven to desperation and helplessness, then he seeks refuge with someone, relying on whom he may feel safe. But where is that refuge to be found? The omnipresent Atman which depends on nothing else to support It is the only Refuge. At first man does not find that. When discrimination and dispassion arise in the course of meditation and spiritual practices, he comes to know it. But in whatever way he may progress on the path of spirituality, everyone is unconsciously awakening Brahman within him. But the means may be different in different cases. Those who have faith in the Personal God have to undergo spiritual practices holding on to that idea. If there is sincerity, through that will come the awakening of the lion of Brahman within. The knowledge of Brahman is the one goal of all beings but the various ideas are the various paths to it. Although the real nature of the Jiva is Brahman, still as he has identification with the qualifying adjunct of the mind, he suffers from all sorts of doubts and difficulties, pleasure and pain. But everyone from Brahmâ down to a blade of grass is advancing towards the realisation of his real nature. And none can escape the round of births and deaths until he realises his identity with Brahman. Getting the human birth, when the desire for freedom becomes very strong, and along with it comes the grace of a person of realisation, then man's desire for Self-knowledge becomes intensified. Otherwise the mind of men given to lust and greed never inclines that way. How should the desire to know Brahman arise in one who has the hankering in his mind for the pleasures of family life, for wealth and for fame? He who is prepared to renounce all, who amid the strong current of the duality of good and evil, happiness and misery, is calm, steady, balanced, and awake to his Ideal, alone endeavours to attain to Self-knowledge. He alone by the might of his own power tears asunder the net of the world. "निर्गच्छति जगज्जालात् पिञ्जरादिव केशरी —Breaking the barriers of Maya, he emerges like a mighty lion."

Disciple: Well then, is it true that without Sannyasa, there can be no knowledge of Brahman?

Swamiji: That is true, a thousand times. One must have both internal and external Sannyasa — renunciation in spirit as also formal renunciation. Shankaracharya, in commenting on the Upanishadic text, "Neither by Tapas (spiritual practice) devoid of the necessary insignia"(Mundaka Upanishad, III. ii. 4.), he said that by practising Sadhana without the external badge of Sannyasa (the Gerua-robe, the staff, Kamandalu, etc.), Brahman, which is difficult to attain, is not realised. Without dispassion for the world, without renunciation, without giving up the desire for enjoyment, absolutely nothing can be accomplished in the spiritual life. "It is not like a sweetmeat in the hands of a child which you can snatch by a trick." (Song of Râmaprâsad.)

Disciple: But, sir, in the course of spiritual practices, that renunciation may come.

Swamiji: Let those to whom it will come gradually have it that way. But why should you sit and wait for that? At once begin to dig the channel which will bring the waters of spirituality to your life. Shri Ramakrishna used to deprecate lukewarmness in spiritual attainments as, for instance, saying that religion would come gradually, and that there was no hurry for it. When one is thirsty, can one sit idle? Does he not run about for water? Because your thirst for spirituality has not come, therefore you are sitting idly. The desire for knowledge has not grown strong, therefore you are satisfied with the little pleasures of family life.

Disciple: Really I do not understand why I don't get that idea of renouncing everything. Do make some way for that, please.

Swamiji: The end and the means are all in your hands. I can only stimulate them. You have read so many scriptures and are serving and associating with such Sadhus who have known Brahman; if even this does not bring the idea of renunciation, then your life is in vain. But it will not be altogether vain; the effects of this will manifest in some way or other in time.

The disciple was much dejected and again said to Swamiji: "Sir, I have come under your refuge, do open the path of Mukti for me – that I may realise the Truth in this body."

Swamiji: What fear is there? Always discriminate – your body, your house, these Jivas and the world are all absolutely unreal like a dream. Always think that this body is only an inert instrument. And the self-contained Purusha within is your real nature. The adjunct of mind is His first and subtle covering, then, there is this body which is His gross, outer covering. The indivisible changeless, self-effulgent Purusha is lying hidden under these delusive veils, therefore your real nature is unknown to you. The direction of the mind which always runs after the senses has to be turned within. The mind has to be killed. The body is but gross – it dies and dissolves into the five elements. But the bundle of mental impressions, which is the mind, does not die soon. It remains for some time in seed-form and then sprouts and grows in the form of a tree – it takes on another physical body and goes the round of birth and death, until Self-knowledge arises. Therefore I say, by meditation and concentration and by the power of philosophical discrimination plunge this mind in the Ocean of Existence-Knowledge-Bliss Absolute. When the mind dies, all limiting adjuncts vanish and you are established in Brahman.

Disciple: Sir, it is so difficult to direct this uncontrolled mind towards Brahman.

Swamiji: Is there anything difficult for the hero? Only men of faint hearts speak so. "वीराणामेव करतलगता मुक्तिः न पुनः कापुरुषाणाम् – Mukti is easy of attainment only to the hero – but not to cowards." Says the Gita (VI. 35), "अभ्यासेन तु कौन्तेय वैराग्येण च गृह्यते – By renunciation and by practice is the mind brought under control, O Arjuna." The Chitta or mind-stuff is like a transparent lake, and the waves which rise in it by the impact of sense-impressions constitute Manas or the mind. Therefore the mind consists of a succession of thought-waves. From these mental waves arises desire. Then that desire transforms itself into will and works through its gross instrument, the body. Again, as work is endless, so its fruits also are endless. Hence the mind is always being tossed by countless myriads of waves – the fruits of work. This mind has to be divested of all modifications (Vrittis) and reconverted into the transparent lake, so that there remains not a single wave of modification in it. Then will Brahman manifest Itself. The scriptures give a glimpse of this state in such passages as: "Then all the knots of the heart are cut asunder", etc. Do you understand?

Disciple: Yes, sir, but meditation must base itself on some object?

Swamiji: You yourself will be the object of your meditation. Think and meditate that you are the omnipresent Atman. "I am neither the body, nor the mind, nor the Buddhi (determinative faculty), neither the gross nor the subtle body" — by this process of elimination, immerse your mind in the transcendent knowledge which is your real nature. Kill the mind by thus plunging it repeatedly in this. Then only you will realise the Essence of Intelligence, or be established in your real nature. Knower and known, meditator and the object meditated upon will then become one, and the cessation of all phenomenal superimpositions will follow. This is styled in the Shâstras as the transcendence of the triad or relative knowledge (Triputibheda). There is no relative or conditioned knowledge in this state. When the Atman is the only knower, by what means can you possibly know It? The Atman is Knowledge, the Atman is Intelligence, the Atman is Sachchidananda. It is through the inscrutable power of Maya, which cannot be indicated as either existent or non-existent, that the relative consciousness has come upon the Jiva who is none other than Brahman. This is generally known as the conscious state. And the state in which this duality of relative existence becomes one in the pure Brahman is called in the scriptures the superconscious state and described in such words as, " स्तिमितसलिलराशिप्रख्यमाख्याविहीनम् — It is like an ocean perfectly at rest and without a name" (*Vivekachudâmani*, 410).

Swamiji spoke these words as if from the profound depths of his realisation of Brahman.

Swamiji: All philosophy and scriptures have come from the plane of relative knowledge of subject and object. But no thought or language of the human mind can fully express the Reality which lies beyond the plane of relative Knowledge! Science, philosophy, etc. are only partial truths. So they can never be the adequate channels of expression for the transcendent Reality. Hence viewed from the transcendent standpoint, everything appears to be unreal — religious creeds, and works, I and thou, and the universe — everything is unreal! Then only it is perceived: "I am the only reality; I am the all-pervading Atman, and I am the proof of my own existence." Where is the room for a separate proof to establish the reality of my existence? I am, as the scriptures say, "नित्यमस्मत्प्रसिद्धम् — Always known to myself as the eternal subject" (*Vivekachudâmani*, 409). I have seen that state, realised it.

You also see and realise it and preach this truth of Brahman to all. Then only will you attain to peace.

While speaking these words, Swamiji's face wore a serious expression and he was lost in thought. After some time he continued: "Realise in your own life this knowledge of Brahman which comprehends all theories and is the rationale of all truths, and preach it to the world. This will conduce to your own good and the good of others as well. I have told you today the essence of all truths; there is nothing higher than this."

Disciple: Sir, now you are speaking of Jnana; but sometimes you proclaim the superiority of Bhakti, sometimes of Karma, and sometimes of Yoga. This confuses our understanding.

Swamiji: Well, the truth is this. The knowledge of Brahman is the ultimate goal – the highest destiny of man. But man cannot remain absorbed in Brahman all the time. When he comes out of it, he must have something to engage himself. At that time he should do such work as will contribute to the real well-being of people. Therefore do I urge you in the service of Jivas in a spirit of oneness. But, my son, such are the intricacies of work, that even great saints are caught in them and become attached. Therefore work has to be done without any desire for results. This is the teaching of the Gita. But know that in the knowledge of Brahman there is no touch of any relation to work. Good works, at the most, purify the mind. Therefore has the commentator Shankara so sharply criticised the doctrine of the combination of Jnana and Karma. Some attain to the knowledge of Brahman by the means of unselfish work. This is also a means, but the end is the realisation of Brahman. Know this thoroughly that the goal of the path of discrimination and of all other modes of practice is the realisation of Brahman.

Disciple: Now, sir, please tell me about the utility of Raja-Yoga and Bhakti-Yoga.

Swamiji: Striving in these paths also some attain to the realisation of Brahman. The path of Bhakti or devotion of God is a slow process, but is easy of practice. In the path of Yoga there are many obstacles; perhaps the mind runs after psychic powers and thus draws you away from attaining your real nature. Only the path of Jnana is of quick fruition and the rationale of all other creeds; hence it is equally esteemed in all countries and all ages. But even in the path of discrimination there is the chance of the mind getting stuck in the interminable net of vain argumentation. Therefore along with it, meditation should be practised. By means of discrimination and meditation, the goal or Brahman has to be reached. One is sure to reach the goal by practising in this way. This, in my opinion, is the easy path ensuring quick success.

Disciple: Now please tell me something about the doctrine of Incarnation of God.

Swamiji: You want to master everything in a day, it seems!

Disciple: Sir, if the doubts and difficulties of the mind be solved in one day, then I shall not have to trouble you time and again.

Swamiji: Those by whose grace the knowledge of Atman, which is extolled so much in the scriptures, is attained in a minute are the moving Tirthas (seats of holiness) – the Incarnations. From their very birth they are knowers of Brahman, and between Brahman and the knower of Brahman there is not the least difference. " – He who knows the Brahman becomes the Brahman" (Mundaka, III. ii. 9). The Atman cannot be known by the mind for It is Itself the Knower – this I have already said. Therefore man's relative knowledge reached up to the Avataras – those who are always established in the Atman. The highest ideal of Ishvara which the human mind can grasp is the Avatara. Beyond this there is no relative knowledge. Such knowers of Brahman are rarely born in the world. And very few people can understand them. They alone are the proof of the truths of the scriptures – the towers of light in the ocean of the world. By the company of such Avataras and by their grace, the darkness of the mind disappears in a trice and realisation flashes immediately in the heart. Why or by what process it comes cannot be ascertained. But it does come. I have seen it happen like that. Shri Krishna spoke the Gita, establishing Himself in the Atman. Those passages of the Gita where He speaks with the word "I", invariably indicate the Atman: "Take refuge in Me alone" means, "Be established in the Atman". This knowledge of the Atman is the highest aim of the Gita. The references to Yoga etc. are but incidental to this realisation of the Atman. Those who have not this knowledge of the Atman are "suicides". "They kill themselves by the clinging to the unreal"; they lose their life in the noose of sense-pleasures. You are also men, and can't you ignore this trash of sensual enjoyment that won't last for two days? Should you also swell the ranks of those who are born and die in utter ignorance? Accept the "beneficial" and discard the "pleasant". Speak of this Atman to all, even to the lowest. By continued speaking your own intelligence also will clear up. And always repeat the great Mantras — "तत्त्वमसि — Thou art That, " सोऽहमस्मि — I am That", " सर्वं खल्विदं ब्रह्म — All this is verily Brahman" — and have the courage of a lion in the heart. What is there to fear? Fear is death — fear is the greatest sin. The human soul, represented by Arjuna, was touched with fear. Therefore Bhagavân Shri Krishna, established in the Atman, spoke to him the teachings of the Gita. Still his fear would not leave him. Later, when Arjuna saw the Universal Form of the Lord, and became established in the Atman, then with all bondages of Karma burnt by the fire of knowledge, he fought the battle.

Disciple: Sir, can a man do work even after realisation?

Swamiji: After realisation, what is ordinarily called work does not persist. It changes its character. The work which the Jnani does only conduces to the well-being of the world. Whatever a man of realisation says or does contributes to the welfare of all. We have observed Shri Ramakrishna; he was, as it were, "देहस्थोऽपि न देहस्थः — In the body, but not of it!" About the motive of the actions of such personages only this can be said: "लोकवत्तु लीलाकैवल्यम् — Everything they do like men, simply by way of sport" (*Brahma-Sutras*, II. i. 33).

XVI

(From the Diary of a Disciple (Shri Sharat Chandra Chakravarty, B.A.))

(Translated from Bengali)

[Place: Belur Math. Year: *1901.*]

The disciple has come to the Math today accompanied by Shri Ranadaprasad Das Gupta, the founder and professor of the Jubilee Art Academy, Calcutta. Ranada Babu is an expert artist, a learned man and an admirer of Swamiji. After the exchange of courtesies Swamiji began to talk with Ranada Babu on various topics relating to art.

Swamiji: I had the opportunity of seeing the beauties of art of nearly every civilised country in the world, but I saw nothing like the development of art which took place in our country during the Buddhistic period. During the régime of the Mogul Emperors also, there was a marked development of art – and the Taj and the Jumma Masjid etc. are standing monuments of that culture.

Art has its origin in the expression of some idea in whatever man produces. Where there is no expression of idea, however much there may be a display of colours and so on, it cannot be styled as true art. Even the articles of everyday use, such as water vessels, or cups and saucers, should be used to express an idea. In the Paris Exhibition I saw a wonderful figure carved in marble. In explanation of the figure, the following words were inscribed underneath: Art unveiling Nature. That is how art sees the inner beauty of nature by drawing away with its own hands the covering veils. The work has been so designed as to indicate that the beauty of nature has not yet become fully unveiled; but the artist is fascinated, as it were, with the beauty of the little that has become manifest. One cannot refrain from praising the sculptor who has tried to express this exquisite idea. You should also try to produce something original like this.

Ranada Babu: Yes, I also have the desire to do some original modelling at leisure. But I meet with no encouragement in this country; it is a poor country and there is want of appreciation.

Swamiji: If you can with your whole heart produce one real thing, if you can rightly express a single idea in art, it must win appreciation in course of time. A real thing never suffers from want of appreciation in this world. It is also heard that some artists have gained appreciation for their works a thousand years after their death!

Ranada Babu: That is true. But we have become so worthless that we haven't got the courage to spend a lot of energy to no purpose. Through these five years' struggle I have succeeded to some extent. Bless me that my efforts be not in vain.

Swamiji: If you set to work in right earnest, then you are sure to be successful. Whoever works at a thing heart and soul not only achieves success in it, but through his absorption in that he also realises the supreme Truth — Brahman. Whoever works at a thing with his whole heart receives help from God.

Ranada Babu: What difference did you find between the art of the West and that of India?

Swamiji: It is nearly the same everywhere. Originality is rarely found. In those countries pictures are painted with the help of models obtained by photographing various objects. But no sooner does one take the help of machinery than all originality vanishes — one cannot give expression to one's ideas. The ancient artists used to evolve original ideas from their brains and try to express them in their paintings. Now the picture being a likeness of photographs, the power of originality and the attempt to develop are getting scarce. But each nation has a characteristic of its own. In its manners and customs, in its mode of living, in painting and sculpture is found the expression of that characteristic idea. For instance, music and dancing in the West are all pointed in their expression. In dance, they look as if jerking the limbs; in instrumental music, the sounds prick the ear like a sword thrust, as it were; so also in vocal music. In this country, on the other hand, the dance has a rolling wave-like movement, and there is the same rounded movement in the varieties of pitch in vocal song. So also in instrumental music. Hence with regard to art also, a different expression is found among different people. People who are very materialistic take nature as their ideal, and try to express in art ideas allied thereto, while the people whose ideal is the transcendent Reality beyond nature try to express that in art through the powers of nature. With regard to the former class of people, nature is the primary basis of art, while with the second class, ideality is the principal motive of artistic development. Thus, though starting with two different ideals in art, they have advanced in it each in its own way. Seeing some paintings in the West you will mistake them for real natural objects. With respect to this country also, when in ancient times sculpture attained a high degree of perfection, if you look at a statue of the period it will make you forget the material world and transport you to a new ideal world. As in Western countries paintings like those of former times are not produced now, so in our country also, attempts to give expression to original ideas in art are no longer seen. For example, the paintings from your art school have got no expression, as it were. It would be well if you try to paint the objects of everyday meditation of the Hindus by giving in them the expression of ancient ideals.

Ranada Babu: I feel much encouraged by your words. I shall try to act up to your suggestions.

Swamiji: Take, for instance, the figure of Mother Kali. In it there is the union of the blissful and the terrible aspects. But in none of the pictures can be seen the true expression of these two aspects. Far from this, there is no attempt to express adequately even one of these two aspects! I have tried to put down some ideas of the terrible aspects of Mother Kali in my English poem, *Kali the Mother*. Can you express those ideas in a picture?

Ranada Babu: Please let me know them.

Swamiji had the poem brought from the library, and began to read it out most impressively to Ranada Babu. Ranada Babu silently listened to the poem, and after a while, as if visualising the figure with his mind's eye, he turned to Swamiji with a frightened look.

Swamiji: Well, will you be able to express this idea in the picture?

Ranada Babu: Yes, I shall try (Ranada Babu began to paint this picture the very next day, but it was never finished, nor shown to Swamiji.); but it turns one's head even to imagine the idea.

Swamiji: After drawing the picture, please show it to me. Then I will tell you about the points necessary to perfect it.

Then Swamiji had the design which he had sketched for the seal (Printed on the title page of this volume.) of the Ramakrishna Mission brought, showed it to Ranada Babu and asked his opinion on it. It depicted a lake in which a lotus blossomed, and there was a swan, and the whole was encircled by a serpent. Ranada Babu at first could not catch the significance of it and asked Swamiji to explain. Swamiji said, "The wavy waters in the picture are symbolic of Karma; the lotus, of Bhakti; and the rising-sun, of Jnana. The encircling serpent is indicative of Yoga and the awakened Kundalini Shakti, while the sun in the picture stands for the Paramâtman (Supreme Self). Therefore the idea of the picture is that by the union of Karma, Jnana, Bhakti, and Yoga, the vision of the Paramatman is obtained."

Ranada Babu kept silent, gratified to hear the *motif* of the picture. After a while he said, "I wish I could learn about art from you!"

Then Swamiji showed to Ranada Babu a drawing, depicting his plan of the future Ramakrishna Temple and Math. Then he began to say, "In the building of this prospective Temple and Math I have the desire to bring together all that is best in Eastern and Western art. I shall try to apply in its construction all the ideas about architecture which I have gathered in my travels all over the world. A big prayer-hall will be built with roof supported on numerous clustered pillars. In its walls, hundreds of lotuses will be in full bloom. It must be big enough to accommodate a thousand persons sitting in meditation. The Ramakrishna temple and prayer-hall should be built together in such a way that from a distance it would taken for a representation of the symbol, "Om". Within the temple there would be a figure of Shri Ramakrishna seated on a swan. On the two sides of the door will be represented the figure of a lion and a lamb licking each other's body in love – expressing the idea that great power and gentleness have become united in love. I have these ideas in my mind; and if I live long enough I shall carry them out. Otherwise future generations will try if they can do it by degrees. It is my opinion that Shri Ramakrishna was born to vivify all branches of art and culture in this country. Therefore this Math has to be built up in such a way that religion, work, learning, Jnana, and Bhakti may spread over the world from this centre. Be you my helpers in this work."

Ranada Babu and the assembled Sannyasins and Brahmacharins listened to Swamiji in mute wonder. After a while Swamiji resumed, "I am discussing the subject at length with you as you are yourself an adept in the line. Now please tell me what you have learnt about the highest ideals of art as the result of your long study of it."

Ranada Babu: What new thing can I tell you? On the contrary, it is you who have opened my eyes on this subject. I have never heard such instructive words on the subject of art in my life. Bless me, sir, that I can work out the ideas that I have got from you.

Then Swamiji got up from his seat and paced the lawn, remarking to the disciple, "He is a very spirited young man."

Disciple: Sir, he is astonished to hear your words.

Swamiji, without answering the disciple, began to hum the lines of a song which Shri Ramakrishna used to sing, "The controlled mind is a great treasure, the philosopher's stone, which yields whatever you want."

After walking a while, Swamiji, washing his face, entered his room with the disciple in company and read the article on Art in the *Enclyclopaedia Britannica* for some time. After finishing it, he began to make fun with the disciple, caricaturing the words and accents of East Bengal.

XVII

(From the Diary of a Disciple (Shri Sharat Chandra Chakravarty, B.A.))

(Translated from Bengali)

[Place: Belur Math. Year: *1901.*]

Swamiji has just returned from East Bengal and Assam a few days back. He is ill, and his feet have swollen. Coming to the Math, the disciple went upstairs and prostrated himself at Swamiji's feet. In spite of his ill health, Swamiji wore his usual smiling face and affectionate look.

Disciple: How are you, Swamiji?

Swamiji: What shall I speak of my health, my son? The body is getting unfit for work day by day. It has been born on the soil of Bengal, and some disease or other is always overtaking it. The physique of this country is not at all good. If you want to do some strenuous work, it cannot bear the strain. But the few days that the body lasts, I will work for you. I shall die in harness.

Disciple: If you give up work for some time and take rest, then you will be all right. Your life means good to the world.

Swamiji: Am I able to sit quiet, my son! Two or three days before Shri Ramakrishna's passing away, She whom he used to call "Kali" entered this body. It is She who takes me here and there and makes me work, without letting me remain quiet or allowing me to look to my personal comforts.

Disciple: Are you speaking metaphorically?

Swamiji: Oh, no; two or three days before his leaving the body, he called me to his side one day, and asking me to sit before him, looked steadfastly at me and fell into Samadhi. Then I really felt that a subtle force like an electric shock was entering my body! In a little while, I also lost outward consciousness and sat motionless. How long I stayed in that condition I do not remember; when consciousness returned I found Shri Ramakrishna shedding tears. On questioning him, he answered me affectionately, "Today, giving you my all, I have become a beggar. With this power you are to do many works for the world's good before you will return." I feel that power is constantly directing me to this or that work. This body has not been made for remaining idle.

Hearing these words with speechless wonder the disciple thought – who knows how common people will take these words? Thereupon he changed the topic and said, "Sir, how did you like our East Bengal?"

Swamiji: I liked it on the whole. The fields, I saw, were rich in crops, the climate also is good, and the scenery on the hill-side is charming. The Brahmaputra Valley is incomparable in its beauty. The people of East Bengal are a little stronger and more active than those of this part. It may be due to their taking plenty of fish and meat. Whatever they do, they do with great persistence. They use a great deal of oil and fat in their food, which is not good, because taking too much of oily and fatty food produces fat in the body.

Disciple: How did you find their religious consciousness?

Swamiji: About religious ideas, I noticed the people are very conservative, and many have turned into fanatics in trying to be liberal in religion. One day a young man brought to me, in the house of Mohini Babu at Dacca, a photograph and said, "Sir, please tell me who he is. Is he an Avatara?" I told him gently many times that I know nothing of it. When even on my telling him three or four times the boy did not cease from his persistent questioning, I was constrained to say at last, "My boy, henceforth take a little nutritious food and then your brain will develop. Without nourishing food, I see your brain has become dried up." At these words the young man may have been much displeased. But what could I do? Unless I spoke like this to the boys, they would turn into madcaps by degrees.

Disciple: In our East Bengal a great many Avataras have cropped up recently.

Swamiji: People may call their Guru an Avatara; they may have any idea of him they like. But Incarnations of God are not born anywhere and everywhere and at all seasons. At Dacca itself I heard there were three or four Avataras!

Disciple: How did you find the women of that side?

Swamiji: The women are very nearly the same everywhere. I found Vaishnavism strong at Dacca. The wife of H__ seemed to be very intelligent. With great care she used to prepare food and send it to me.

Disciple: I heard you have been to Nag Mahashaya's place.

Swamiji: Yes, going so far, should I not visit the birthplace of such a great soul? His wife fed me with many delicacies prepared by her own hand. The house is charming, like a peace retreat. There I took a swimming bath in a village pond. After that I had such a sound sleep that I woke at half past two in the afternoon. Of the few days I had sound sleep in my life, that in Nag Mahashaya's house was one. Rising from sleep I had a plentiful repast. Nag Mahashaya's wife presented me a cloth which I tied round my head as a turban and started for Dacca. I found that the photograph of Nag Mahashaya was being worshipped there. The place where his remains lie interred ought to be well kept. Even now it is not as it should be.

Disciple: The people of that part have not been able to appreciate Nag Mahashaya.

Swamiji: How can ordinary people appreciate a great man like him? Those who had his company are blessed indeed.

Disciple: What did you see at Kâmâkhyâ?

Swamiji: The Shillong hills are very beautiful. There I met Sir Henry Cotton, the Chief Commissioner of Assam. He asked me, "Swamiji, after travelling through Europe and America, what have you come to see here in these distant hills?" Such a good and kind-hearted man as Sir Henry Cotton is rarely found. Hearing of my illness, he sent the Civil Surgeon and inquired after my health mornings and evenings. I could not do much lecturing there, because my health was very bad. On the way Nitai served and looked after me nicely.

Disciple: What did you find the religious ideas of that part to be?

Swamiji: It is the land of the Tantras. I heard of one "Hankar Deva" who is worshipped there as an Avatara. I heard his sect is very wide-spread. I could not ascertain if "Hankar Deva" was but another form of the name Shankaracharya. They are monks — perhaps Tântrika Sannyasins, or perhaps one of the Shankara sects.

Disciple: The people of East Bengal have not been able to appreciate you as is the case with Nag Mahashaya.

Swamiji: Whether they appreciate me or not, the people there are more active and energetic than those of these parts. In time it will develop more. What are nowadays known as refined or civilised ways have not yet thoroughly entered those parts. Gradually they will. In all times, etiquette and fashion spread to the countryside from the capital. And this is happening in East Bengal also. The land that has produced a great soul like Nag Mahashaya is blessed and has a hopeful future. By the light of his personality Eastern Bengal is radiant.

Disciple: But, sir, ordinary people did not know him as a great soul. He hid himself in great obscurity.

Swamiji: There they used to make much fuss about my food and say, "Why should you eat that food or eat from the hands of such and such?" — and so on. To which I had to reply, "I am a Sannyasin and a mendicant friar and what need have I to observe so much outward formality with regard to food etc.? Do not your scriptures say, " चरेन्माधुकरीं वृत्तिमपि म्लेच्छकुलादपि — One should beg one's food from door to door, ay even from the house of an outcast"? But of course external forms are necessary in the beginning, for the inner realisation of religion, in order to make the truth of the scriptures practical in one's life. Haven't you heard of Shri Ramakrishna's story of "wringing out the almanac for water"? Outward forms and observances are only for the manifestation of the great inner powers of man. The object of all scriptures is to awaken those inner powers and make him understand and realise his real nature. The means are of the nature of ordinances and prohibitions. If you lose sight of the ideal fight over the means only, what will it avail? In every country I have visited, I find this fighting over the means going on, and people have no eye on the ideal. Shri Ramakrishna came to show the truth of this.

Realisation of the truth is the essential thing. Whether you bathe in the Ganga for a thousand years or live on vegetable food for a like period, unless it helps towards the manifestation of the Self, know that it is all of no use. If on the other hand, any one can realise the Atman, without the observance of outward forms, then that very non-observance of forms is the best means. But even after the realisation of Atman, one should observe outward forms to a certain extent for setting an example to the people. The thing is you must make the mind steadfast on something. If it is steadfast on one object, it attains to concentration, that is, its other modifications die out and there is a uniform flow in one direction. Many become wholly preoccupied with the outward forms and observances merely and fail to direct their mind to thoughts of the Atman! If you remain day and night within the narrow groove of ordinances and prohibitions, how will there be any expression of the soul? The more one has advanced in the realisation of the Atman, the less is he dependent on the observances of forms. Shankaracharya also has said, " निस्त्रैगुण्ये पथि विचरतां को विधिः को निषेधः – Where is there any ordinance or prohibition for him whose mind is always above the play of the Gunas?" Therefore the essential truth is realisation. Know that to be the goal. Each distinct creed is but a way to the Truth. The test of progress is the amount of renunciation that one has attained. Where you find the attraction for lust and wealth considerably diminished, to whatever creed he may belong, know that his inner spirit is awakening. The door of Self-realisation has surely opened for him. On the contrary if you observe a thousand outward rules and quote a thousand scriptural texts, still, if it has not brought the spirit of renunciation in you, know that your life is in vain. Be earnest over this realisation and set your heart on it. Well, you have read enough of scriptures. But tell me, of what avail has it been? Some perhaps thinking of money have become millionaires, whereas you have become a Pundit by thinking of scriptures. But both are bondages. Attain the supreme knowledge and go beyond Vidyâ and Avidyâ, relative knowledge and ignorance.

Disciple: Sir, through your grace I understand it all, but my past Karma does not allow me to assimilate these teachings.

Swamiji: Throw aside your Karma and all such stuff. If it is a truth that by your own past action you have got this body; then, nullifying the effects of evil works by good works, why should you not be a Jivanmukta in this very body? Know that freedom or Self-Knowledge is in your own hands. In real knowledge there is no touch of work. But those who work after being Jivanmuktas do so for the good of others. They do not look to the results of works. No seed of desire finds any room in their mind. And strictly speaking it is almost impossible to work like that for the good of the world from the householder's position. In the whole of Hindu scriptures there is the single instance of King Janaka in this respect. But you nowadays want to pose as Janakas (lit. fathers) in every home by begetting children year after year, while he was without the body-consciousness!

Disciple: Please bless me that I may attain Self-realisation in this very life.

Swamiji: What fear? If there is sincerity of spirit, I tell you, for a certainty, you will attain it in this very life. But manly endeavour is wanted. Do you know what it is? "I shall certainly attain Self-knowledge. Whatever obstacles may come, I shall certainly overcome them" – a firm determination like this is Purushakâra. "Whether my mother, father, friends, brothers, wife, and children live or die, whether this body remains or goes, I shall never turn back till I attain to the vision of the Atman" — this resolute endeavour to advance towards one's goal, setting at naught all other considerations, is termed manly endeavour. Otherwise, endeavour for creature comforts even beasts and birds show. Man has got this body simply to realise Self-knowledge. If you follow the common run of people in the world and float with the general current, where then is your manliness? Well, the common people are going to the jaws of death! But you have come to conquer it! Advance like a hero. Don't be thwarted by anything. How many days will this body last, with its happiness and misery? When you have got the human body, then rouse the Atman within and say — I have reached the state of fearlessness! Say — I am the Atman in which my lower ego has become merged for ever. Be perfect in this idea; and then as long as the body endures, speak unto others this message of fearlessness: "Thou art That", "Arise, awake, and stop not till the goal is reached!" If you can achieve this, then shall I know that you are really a tenacious East Bengal man.

XVIII

(From the Diary of a Disciple (Shri Sharat Chandra Chakravarty, B.A.))

(Translated from Bengali)

[Place: Belur Math. Year: *1901.*]

Swamiji is in indifferent health since his return to the Math from the Shillong Hills. His feet have swollen. All this has made his brother-disciples very anxious. At the request of Swami Niranjanananda, Swamiji has agreed to take Âyurvedic medicine. He is to begin this treatment from next Tuesday and entirely give up taking water and salt. Today is Sunday. The disciple asked him, "Sir, it is terribly hot now and you drink water very frequently; it will be unbearable for you now to stop taking water altogether for this treatment."

Swamiji: What do you say? I shall make a firm resolve, on the morning of the day I shall begin this treatment, not to take any water. After that no water shall pass down the throat any more. For three weeks not a drop of water shall be able to go down the throat. The body is but an outer covering of the mind and whatever the mind will dictate to it, it will have to carry out. So there is nothing to be afraid of. At the request of Niranjan I have to undergo this treatment. Well, I cannot be indifferent to the request of my brother-disciples.

It is now about ten o'clock. Swamiji cheerfully raised the topic of his future Math for women, saying, "With the Holy Mother as the centre of inspiration, a Math is to be established on the eastern bank of the Ganga. As Brahmacharins and Sâdhus will be trained in this Math here, so in the other Math also, Brahmacharinis and Sâdhvis will be trained."

Disciple: Sir, history does not tell us of any Maths for women in India in ancient times. Only during the Buddhistic period one hears of Maths for women; but from it in course of time many corruptions arose. The whole country was overrun by great evil practices.

Swamiji: It is very difficult to understand why in this country so much difference is made between men and women, whereas the Vedanta declares that one and the same conscious Self is present in all beings. You always criticise the women, but say what have you done for their uplift? Writing down Smritis etc., and binding them by hard rules, the men have turned the women into mere manufacturing machines! If you do not raise the women, who are the living embodiment of the Divine Mother, don't think that you have any other way to rise.

Disciple: Women are a bondage and a snare to men. By their Maya they cover the knowledge and dispassion of men. It is for this, I suppose, that scriptural writers hint that knowledge and devotion are difficult of attainment to them.

Swamiji: In what scriptures do you find statements that women are not competent for knowledge and devotion? In the period of degradation, when the priests made other castes incompetent for the study of the Vedas, they deprived the women also of all their rights. Otherwise you will find that in the Vedic or Upanishadic age Maitreyi, Gârgi, and other ladies of revered memory have taken the places of Rishis through their skill in discussing about Brahman. In an assembly of a thousand Brahmanas who were all erudite in the Vedas, Gargi boldly challenged Yâjnavalkya in a discussion about Brahman. Since such ideal women were entitled to spiritual knowledge, why shall not the women have the same privilege now? What has happened once can certainly happen again. History repeats itself. All nations have attained greatness by paying proper respect to women. That country and that nation which do not respect women have never become great, nor will ever be in future. The principal reason why your race has so much degenerated is that you have no respect for these living images of Shakti. Manu says, "Where women are respected, there the gods delight; and where they are not, there all works and efforts come to naught." (Manu, III. 56.) There is no hope of rise for that family or country where there is no estimation of women, where they live in sadness. For this reason, they have to be raised first; and an ideal Math has to be started for them.

Disciple: Sir, when you first returned from the West, in your lecture at the Star Theatre you sharply criticised the Tantras. Now by your supporting the worship of women, as taught in the Tantras, you are contradicting yourself.

Swamiji: I denounced only the present corrupted form of Vâmâchâra of the Tantras. I did not denounce the Mother-worship of the Tantras, or even the real Vamachara. The purport of the Tantras is to worship women in a spirit of Divinity. During the downfall of Buddhism, the Vamachara became very much corrupted, and that corrupted form obtains to the present day. Even now the Tantra literature of India is influenced by those ideas. I denounced only these corrupt and horrible practices — which I do even now. I never objected to the worship of women who are the living embodiment of Divine Mother, whose external manifestations, appealing to the senses have maddened men, but whose internal manifestations, such as knowledge, devotion, discrimination and dispassion make man omniscient, of unfailing purpose, and a knower of Brahman. " – She, when pleased, becomes propitious and the cause of the freedom of man" (*Chandi*, I. 57). Without propitiating the Mother by worship and obeisance, not even Brahmâ and Vishnu have the power to elude Her grasp and attain to freedom. Therefore for the worship of these family goddesses, in order to manifest the Brahman within them, I shall establish the women's Math.

Disciple: It may be a good idea but where will you get the women inmates? With the present hard restrictions of society, who will permit the ladies of their household to join your Math?

Swamiji: Why so? Even now there are women disciples of Shri Ramakrishna. With their help I shall start this Math. The Holy Mother will be their central figure and the wives and daughters of the devotees of Shri Ramakrishna will be its first inmates. For they will easily appreciate the usefulness of such a Math. After that, following their example, many householders will help in their noble work.

Disciple: The devotees of Shri Ramakrishna will certainly join this work. But I don't think the general public will help in this work.

Swamiji: No great work has been done in the world without sacrifice. Who on seeing the tiny sprout of the banyan can imagine that in course of time it will develop into a gigantic banyan tree? At present I shall start the Math in this way. Later on you will see that after a generation or two people of this country will appreciate the worth of this Math. My women disciples will lay down their lives for it. Casting off fear and cowardice, you also be helpers in this noble mission and hold this high ideal before all. You will see, it will shed its lustre over the whole country in time.

Disciple: Sir, please tell me all about your plan of this Math for women.

Swamiji: On the other side of the Ganga a big plot of land will be acquired, where unmarried girls or Brahmacharini widows will live; devout married women will also be allowed to stay now and then. Men will have no concern with this Math. The elderly Sadhus of the Math will manage the affairs of this Math from a distance. There shall be a girls' school attached to this women's Math, in which religious scriptures, literature, Sanskrit grammar, and even some amount of English should be taught. Other matters such as sewing, culinary art, rules of domestic work, and upbringing of children, will also be taught while Japa, worship, meditation, etc. shall form an indispensable part of the teaching. Those who will be able to live here permanently, renouncing home and family ties, will be provided with food and clothing from the Math. Those who will not be able to do that will be allowed to study in this Math as day-scholars. With the permission of the head of the Math, the latter will be allowed even to stay in the Math occasionally, and during such stay will be maintained by the Math. The elder Brahmacharinis will take charge of the training of the girl students in Brahmacharya. After five or six years' training in this Math, the guardians of the girls may marry them. If deemed fit for Yoga and religious life, with the permission of the guardians they will be allowed to stay in this Math, taking the vow of celibacy. These celibate nuns will in time be the teachers and preachers of the Math. In villages and towns they will open centres and strive for the spread of female education. Through such devout preachers of character there will be the real spread of female education in the country. So long as the students will remain in association with this Math, they must observe Brahmacharya as the basic ideal of this Math.

Spirituality, sacrifice, and self-control will be the motto of the pupils of this Math, and service or Sevâ-dharma the vow of their life. In view of such ideal lives, who will not respect and have faith in them? If the life of the women of this country be moulded in such fashion, then only will there be the reappearance of such ideal characters as Sitâ, Sâvitri and Gârgi. To what straits the strictures of local usages have reduced the women of this country, rendering them lifeless and inert, you could understand if only you visited the Western countries. You alone are responsible for this miserable condition of the women, and it rests with you also to raise them again. Therefore I say, set to work. What will it do to memorise a few religious books like the Vedas and so on?

Disciple: Sir, if the girl students after being trained in this Math marry, how will one find ideal characters in them? Will it not be better if the rule is made that those who will be educated in this Math shall not marry?

Swamiji: Can that be brought about all at once? They must be given education and left to themselves. After that they will act as they think best. Even after marriage and entering the world, the girls educated as above will inspire their husbands with noble ideals and be the mothers of heroic sons. But there must be this rule that the guardians of the students in the women's Math must not even think of marrying them before they attain the age of fifteen.

Disciple: Sir, then those girls will not command reputation in society. Nobody would like to marry them.

Swamiji: Why will not they be wanted in marriage? You have not yet understood the trend of society. These learned and accomplished girls will never be in want of bridegrooms. Society nowadays does not follow the texts recommending child-marriage nor will do so in future. Even now don't you see?

Disciple: But there is sure to be a violent opposition against this in the beginning.

Swamiji: Let it be. What is there to be afraid of in that? Opposition to a righteous work initiated with moral courage will only awaken the moral power of the initiators the more. That which meets with no obstruction, no opposition, only takes men to the path of moral death. Struggle is the sign of life.

Disciple: Yes, sir.

Swamiji: In the highest reality of the Parabrahman, there is no distinction of sex. We notice this only in the relative plane. And the more the mind becomes introspective, the more that idea of difference vanishes. Ultimately, when the mind is wholly merged in the homogeneous and undifferentiated Brahman, such ideas as this is a man or that a woman do not remain at all. We have actually seen this in the life of Shri Ramakrishna. Therefore do I say that though outwardly there may be difference between men and women, in their real nature there is none. Hence, if a man can be a knower of Brahman, why cannot a woman attain to the same knowledge? Therefore I was saying that if even one amongst the women became a knower of Brahman, then by the radiance of her personality thousands of women would be inspired and awakened to truth, and great well-being of the country and society would ensue. Do you understand?

Disciple: Sir, your teachings have opened my eyes today.

Swamiji: Not fully yet. When you realise that all-illumining reality of the Atman, then you will see that this idea of sex-distinction has vanished altogether, then only will you look upon women as the veritable manifestation of Brahman. We have seen in Shri Ramakrishna how he had this idea of divine motherhood in every woman, of whatever caste she might be, or whatever might be her worth. It is because I have seen this that I ask you all so earnestly to do likewise and open girls' schools in every village and try to uplift them. If the women are raised, then their children will by their noble actions glorify the name of the country — then will culture, knowledge, power, and devotion awaken in the land.

Disciple: But, sir, contrary results appear to have come out of the present female education. With just a smattering of education, they take merely to the Western modes of living, but it is not clear how far they are advancing in the spirit of renunciation, self-control, austerity, Brahmacharya and other qualities conducive to Brahmajnana.

Swamiji: In the beginning a few mistakes like that are unavoidable. When a new idea is preached in the country, some, failing to grasp it properly, go wrong in that way. But what matters it to the well-being of society at large? Well, those who are pioneers of the little bit of female education that now obtains in the country were undoubtedly very great-hearted. But the truth is that some defect or other must creep into that learning or culture which is not founded on a religious basis. But now female education is to be spread with religion as its centre. All other training should be secondary to religion. Religious training, the formation of character and observance of the vow of celibacy — these should be attended to. In the female education which has obtained up till now in India, it is religion that has been made a secondary concern, hence those defects you were speaking of have crept in. But no blame attaches therefore to the women. Reformers having proceeded to start female education without being Brahmacharins themselves have stumbled like that. Founders of all good undertakings, before they launch on their desired work, must attain to the knowledge of the Atman through rigorous self-discipline. Otherwise defects are bound to occur in their work.

Disciple: Yes, sir, it is observed that many educated women spend their time in reading novels and so on; but in East Bengal even with education women have not given up their religious observances. Is it so here in this part?

Swamiji: In every country, nations have their good and bad sides. Ours is to do good works in our lives and hold an example before others. No work succeeds by condemnation. It only repels people. Let anybody say what he likes, don't contradict him. In this world of Maya, whatever work you will take up will be attended with some defect. " सर्वारम्भा हि दोषेण धूमेनाग्निरिवावृताः — All works are covered with defects as fire is with smoke" (Gita, XVIII. 48). Every fire has a chance of being attended with smoke. But will you, on that account, sit inactive? As far as you can, you must go on doing good work.

Disciple: What is this good work?

Swamiji: Whatever helps in the manifestation of Brahman is good work. Any work can be done so as to help, if not directly, at least indirectly, the manifestation of the Atman. But following the path laid down by the Rishis, that knowledge of the Atman manifests quickly; on the contrary, the doing of works which have been indicated by the scriptural writers as wrong, brings only bondage of the soul and sometimes this bondage of delusion does not vanish even in many lives. But in all ages and climes, freedom is sure to be attained by Jivas ultimately. For the Atman is the real nature of the Jiva. Can anybody give up his own nature? If you fight with your shadow for a thousand years, can you drive it away from you? — it will always remain with you.

Disciple: But, sir, according to Shankara, Karma is antagonistic to Jnana. He has variously refuted the intermingling of Jnana and Karma. So how can Karma be helpful to the manifestation of Jnana?

Swamiji: Shankara after saying so has again described Karma as indirect help to the manifestation of Jnana and the means for the purification of the mind. But I do not contradict his conclusion that in transcendent knowledge there is no touch of any work whatsoever. So long as man is within the realm of the consciousness of action, agent, and the result of action, he is powerless to sit idle without doing some work. So, as work is thus ingrained in the very nature of man, why don't you go on doing such works as are helpful to the manifestation of the knowledge of the Atman? That all work is the effect of ignorance may be true from the absolute standpoint, but within the sphere of relative consciousness it has a great utility. When you will realise the Atman, the doing or non-doing of work will be within your control, and whatever you will do in that state will be good work, conducive to the well-being of Jivas and the world. With the manifestation of Brahman, even the breath you draw will be to the good of Jiva. Then you will no longer have to work by means of conscious planning. Do you understand?

Disciple: Yes, it is a beautiful conclusion reconciling Karma and Jnana from the Vedantic standpoint.

At this time, the bell for supper rang, and the disciple, before going to partake of it, prayed with folded hands, "Bless me, sir, that I may attain to the knowledge of Brahman in this very life." Swamiji placing his hand on the disciple's head said, "Have no fear, my son. You are not like ordinary worldly men – neither householders, nor exactly Sannyasins – but quite a new type."

XIX

(From the Diary of a Disciple (Shri Sharat Chandra Chakravarty, B.A.))

(Translated from Bengali)

[Place: Belur Math. Year: *1901.*]

Swamiji is in indifferent health. At the earnest request of Swami Niranjanananda he has been taking Ayurvedic medicines for six or seven days. According to this treatment, the drinking of water is strictly forbidden. He has to appease his thirst with milk.

The disciple has come to the Math early in the day. Swamiji on seeing him spoke with affection, "Oh, you have come? Well done, I was thinking of you."

Disciple: I hear that you are living on milk for the last six or seven days.

Swamiji: Yes, at the earnest entreaty of Niranjan, I had to take to this medicine! I cannot disregard their request.

Disciple: You were in the habit of taking water very frequently. How could you give it up altogether?

Swamiji: When I heard that according to this treatment water had to be given up, I made a firm resolve immediately not to take water. Now the idea of drinking water does not even occur to the mind.

Disciple: The treatment is doing you good I hope?

Swamiji: That I don't know. I am simply obeying the orders of my brother-disciples.

Disciple: I think that indigenous drugs such as the Vaidyas use, are very well-suited to our constitution.

Swamiji: My idea is that it is better even to die under the treatment of a scientific doctor than expect recovery from the treatment of laymen who know nothing of modern science, but blindly go by the ancient books, without gaining a mastery of the subject – even though they may have cured a few cases.

Swamiji cooked certain dishes, one of which was prepared with vermicelli. When the disciple, who partook of it, asked Swamiji what it was, he replied, "It is a few English earthworms which I have brought dried from London." This created laughter among those present at the expense of the disciple. Despite his spare food and scanty sleep, Swamiji is very active. A few days ago, a new set of the *Encyclopaedia Britannica* had been bought for the Math. Seeing the new shining volumes, the disciple said to Swamiji, "It is almost impossible to read all these books in a single lifetime." He was unaware that Swamiji had already finished ten volumes and had begun the eleventh.

Swamiji: What do you say? Ask me anything you like from these ten volumes, and I will answer you all.

The disciple asked in wonder, "Have you read all these books?"

Swamiji: Why should I ask you to question me otherwise?

Being examined, Swamiji not only reproduced the sense, but at places the very language of the difficult topics selected from each volume. The disciple, astonished, put aside the books, saying, "This is not within human power!"

Swamiji: Do you see, simply by the observance of strict Brahmacharya (continence) all learning can be mastered in a very short time – one has an unfailing memory of what one hears or knows but once. It is owing to this want of continence that everything is on the brink of ruin in our country.

Disciple: Whatever you may say, sir, the manifestation of such superhuman power cannot be the result of mere Brahmacharya, something else there must be.

Swamiji did not say anything in reply.

Then Swamiji began to explain lucidly to the disciple the arguments and conclusions about the difficult points in all philosophies. In course of the conversation Swami Brahmananda entered the room and said to the disciple, "You are a nice man! Swamiji is unwell, and instead of trying to keep his mind cheerful by light talk, you are making him talk incessantly, raising the most abstruse subjects!" The disciple was abashed. But Swamiji said to Swami Brahmananda, "Keep your regulation of Ayurvedic treatment aside. These are my children; and if my body goes in teaching them, I don't care." After this, some light talk followed. Then arose the topic of the place of Bhâratchandra in Bengali literature. From the beginning Swamiji began to ridicule Bharatchandra in various ways and satirised the life, manners, marriage-customs, and other usages of society at the time of Bharatchandra, who was an advocate of child-marriage. He expressed the opinion that the poems of Bharatchandra, being full of bad taste and obscenities, had not found acceptance in any cultured society except in Bengal, and he said, "Care should be taken that such books do not come into the hands of boys." Then raising the topic of Michael Madhusudan Dutt, he added, "That was a wonderful genius born in your province. There is not another epic in Bengali literature like the *Meghnâdbadh*, no mistake in that; and it is difficult to come across a poem like that in the whole of modern European literature."

Disciple: But, sir, I think Michael was very fond of a bombastic style.

Swamiji: Well, if anybody in your country does anything new, you at once hoot him. First examine well what he is saying, but instead of that, the people of the country will chase after anything which is not quite after the old modes. For example, in order to bring to ridicule this *Meghnabadh Kâvya*, which is the gem of Bengali literature, the parody of *Chhuchhundaribadh Kâvya* (The Death of a Mole) was written. They may caricature as much as they like, it does not matter. But the *Meghnadbadh Kavya* still stands unshaken in its reputation like the Himalayas while the opinions and writings of carping critics who are busy picking holes in it have been washed away into oblivion. What will the vulgar public understand of this epic Michael has written in such a vigorous diction and an original metre? And at the present time Girish Babu is writing wonderful books in a new metre which your overwise Pundits are criticising and finding fault with. But does G.C. care for that? People will appreciate the book afterwards.

Thus speaking on the subject of Michael he said, "Go and get the *Meghnadbadh Kavya* from the library downstairs." On the disciple's bringing it he said, "Now read, let me see how you can read it."

The disciple read a portion, but the reading not being to the liking of Swamiji, he took the book and showed him how to read and asked him to read again. Then he asked him, "Now, can you say which portion of the Kavya is best?" The disciple failing to answer, Swamiji said, "That portion of the book which describes how Indrajit has been killed in battle and Mandodari, beside herself with grief, is dissuading Râvana from the battle – but Ravana casting off forcibly from his mind the grief for his son is firmly resolved on battle like a great hero, and forgetting in a fury of rage and vengeance all about his wife and children, is ready to rush out for battle – that is the most finely conceived portion of the book. Come what may, I shall not forget my duty, whether the world remains or dissolves-these are the words of a great hero. Inspired by such feelings, Michael has written that portion."

Saying this, Swamiji opened the particular passage and began to read it in the most impressive manner.

XX

(From the Diary of a Disciple (Shri Sharat Chandra Chakravarty, B.A.))

(Translated from Bengali)

[Place: Belur Math. Year: *1901.*]

Swamiji is much better under the Ayurvedic treatment. The disciple is at the Math. While attending on Swamiji, he asked, "The Atman is all-pervading, the very life of the life of all beings, and so very near. Still why is It not perceived?"

Swamiji: Do you see yourself that you have eyes? When others speak of the eyes, then you are reminded that you have got eyes. Again when dust or sand enters into them and sets up an irritation, then you feel quite well that you have got eyes. Similarly the realisation of this universal Atman which is inner than the innermost is not easily attained. Reading from scriptures or hearing from the lips of the preceptor, one has some idea of It, but when the hard lashes of the bitter sorrow and pain of the world make the heart sore, when on the death of one's near and dear relatives, man thinks himself helpless, when the impenetrable and insurmountable darkness about the future life agitates his mind, then does the Jiva pant for a realisation of the Atman. Therefore is sorrow helpful to the knowledge of the Atman. But one should remember the bitter lesson of experience. Those who die, merely suffering the woes of life like cats and dogs, are they men? He is a man who even when agitated by the sharp interaction of pleasure and pain is discriminating, and knowing them to be of an evanescent nature, becomes passionately devoted to the Atman. This is all the difference between men and animals. That which is nearest is least observed. The Atman is the nearest of the near, therefore the careless and unsteady mind of man gets no clue to It. But the man who is alert, calm, self-restrained, and discriminating, ignores the external world and diving more and more into the inner world, realises the glory of the Atman and becomes great. Then only he attains to the knowledge of the Atman and realises the truth of such scriptural texts as, "I am the Atman", "Thou art That, O Shvetaketu," and so on. Do you understand?

Disciple: Yes, sir. But why this method of attaining Self-knowledge through the path of pain and suffering? Instead of all this, it would have been well if there had been no creation at all. We were all at one time identified with Brahman. Why then this desire for creation on the path of Brahman? Why again this going forth of the Jiva (who is no other than Brahman) along the path of birth and death, amidst the interaction of the dualities of life?

Swamiji: When a man is intoxicated, he sees many hallucinations; but when the intoxication goes off, he understands them as the imaginations of a heated brain. Whatever you see of this creation which is without a beginning, but has an end, is only an effect of your state of intoxication; when that passes off, such questions will not arise at all.

Disciple: Then is there no reality in the creation, and preservation, etc. of the Universe?

Swamiji: Why should not there be? So long as you identify yourself with the body and have the ego-consciousness, all these will remain. But when you are bereft of the body-consciousness and devoted to the Atman and live in the Atman, then with respect to you none of these will remain, and such questions as whether there is any creation or birth or death will have no room. Then you will have to say —

कव गतं केन वा नीतं कुत्र लीनमीदं जगत् ।
अधुनैव मया दृष्टं नासित किं महदद्भुतम् ॥

— "Where is it gone, by whom is it taken, wherein is the world merged? It was just observed by me and is it non-existent now? What a wonder!" (*Vivekachudâmani* 483).

Disciple: If there is no knowledge of the existence of the universe, how can it be said, "Wherein is the world merged?"

Swamiji: Because one has to express the idea in language, therefore that mode of expression has been used. The author has tried to express in thought and language about the state where thought or language cannot reach, and therefore he has stated the fact that the world is wholly unreal, in a relative mode like the above. The world has no absolute reality which only belongs to Brahman, which is beyond the reach of mind and speech. Say what more you have to ask. Today I will put an end to all your arguments.

The bell of the evening service in the worship-room rang at the time, and everybody made for it. But the disciple stayed in Swamiji's room, noticing which Swamiji said, "Won't you go to the worship-room?"

Disciple: I should like to stay here.

Swamiji: All right.

After some time the disciple looking outside of the room said, "It is the new-moon night and all the quarters are overspread with darkness. It is the night for the worship of Mother Kali."

Swamiji without saying anything gazed at the eastern sky for some time and said, "Do you see what a mysterious and solemn beauty there is in this darkness!" Saying this and continuing to look at the dense mass of darkness, he stood enwrapt. After some minutes had passed, Swamiji slowly began to sing a Bengali song, "O Mother, in deep darkness flashes Thy formless beauty", etc. After the song Swamiji entered his room and sat down with an occasional word like "Mother, Mother", or "Kali, Kali", on his lips.

Uneasy at Swamiji's profoundly abstracted mood, the disciple said, "Now, sir, please speak with me."

Swamiji smilingly said, "Can you fathom the beauty and profundity of the Atman whose external manifestation is so sweet and beautiful?" The disciple wished for a change of topic, noticing which, Swamiji began another song of Kali: "O Mother, Thou flowing stream of nectar, in how many forms and aspects dost Thou play in manifestation!" After the song he said, "This Kali is Brahman in manifestation. Haven't you heard Shri Ramakrishna's illustration of the 'snake moving and the snake at rest' (representing the dynamic and static aspects of the same thing)?"

Disciple: Yes, sir.

Swamiji: This time, when I get well, I shall worship the Mother with my heart's blood, then only will She be pleased. Your Raghunandan also says like that. The Mother's child shall be a hero, a Mahâvira. In unhappiness, sorrow, death, and desolation, the Mother's child shall always remain fearless.

XXI

(From the Diary of a Disciple (Shri Sharat Chandra Chakravarty, B.A.))

(Translated from Bengali)

[Place: Belur Math. Year: 1901.]

Swamiji is staying at the Math nowadays. His health is not very good, but he goes out for a walk in the mornings and evenings. The disciple, after bowing at the feet of Swamiji, inquired about his health.

Swamiji: Well, this body is in such a pitiable condition, but none of you are stepping forward to help in my work! What shall I do single-handed? This time the body has come out of the soil of Bengal, so can it bear the strain of much work? You who come here are pure souls; and if you do not become my helpers in this work, what shall I do alone?

Disciple: Sir, these self-sacrificing Brahmacharins and Sannyasins are standing behind you, and I think that each one of them can devote his life to your work – still why do you speak in this way?

Swamiji: Well, I want a band of young Bengal – who alone are the hope of this country. My hope of the future lies in the youths of character – intelligent, renouncing all for the service of others, and obedient – who can sacrifice their lives in working out my ideas and thereby do good to themselves and the country at large. Otherwise, boys of the common run are coming in groups and will come. Dullness is written on their faces – their hearts are devoid of energy, their bodies feeble and unfit for work, and minds devoid of courage. What work will be done by these? If I get ten or twelve boys with the faith of Nachiketâ, I can turn the thoughts and pursuits of this country in a new channel.

Disciple: Sir, so many young men are coming to you, and do you find none among them of such a nature?

Swamiji: Among those who appear to me to be of good calibre, some have bound themselves by matrimony; some have sold themselves for the acquisition of worldly name, fame, or wealth; while some are of feeble bodies. The rest, who form the majority, are unable to receive any high idea.

You are no doubt fit to receive my high ideas, but you are not able to work them out in the practical field. For these reasons sometimes an anguish comes into the mind, and I think that taking this human body, I could not do much work through untowardness of fortune. Of course, I have not yet wholly given up hope, for, by the will of God, from among these very boys may arise in time great heroes of action and spirituality who will in future work out my ideas.

Disciple: It is my firm belief that your broad and liberal ideas must find universal acceptance some day or other. For I see they are all-sided and infusing vigour into every department of thought and activity. And the people of the country are accepting, either overtly or covertly, your ideas, and teaching them to the people.

Swamiji: What matters it if they acknowledge my name or not? It is enough if they accept my ideas. Ninety-nine per cent of the Sadhus, even after renouncing lust and wealth, get bound at the last by the desire of name and fame. "Fame . . . that last infirmity of noble mind" — haven't you read? We shall have to work, giving up altogether all desire for results. People will call us both good and bad. But we shall have to work like lions, keeping the ideal before us, without caring whether "the wise ones praise or blame us".

Disciple: What ideal should we follow now?

Swamiji: You have now to make the character of Mahâvira your ideal. See how at the command of Râmachandra he crossed the ocean. He had no care for life or death! He was a perfect master of his senses and wonderfully sagacious. You have now to build your life on this great ideal of personal service. Through that, all other ideals will gradually manifest in life. Obedience to the Guru without questioning, and strict observance of Brahmacharya — this is the secret of success. As on the one hand Hanumân represent the ideal of service, so on the other hand he represents leonine courage, striking the whole world with awe. He has not the least hesitation in sacrificing his life for the good of Rama. A supreme indifference to everything except the service of Rama, even to the attainment of the status of Brahmâ and Shiva, the great World-Gods! Only the carrying out of Shri Rama's best is the one vow of this life! Such whole-hearted devotion is wanted. Playing on the Khol and Kartâl and dancing in the frenzy of Kirtana has degenerated the whole people. They are, in the first place, a race of dyspeptics — and if in addition to this they dance and jump in that way, how can they bear the strain? In trying to imitate the highest Sâdhana, the preliminary qualification for which is absolute purity, they have been swallowed in dire Tamas. In every district and village you may visit, you will find only the sound of the Khol and Kartâl! Are not drums made in the country? Are not trumpets and kettle-drums available in India? Make the boys hear the deep-toned sound of these instruments. Hearing from boyhood the sound of these effeminate forms of music and listening to the kirtana, the country is well-nigh converted into a country of women. What more degradation can you expect? Even the poet's imagination fails to draw this picture! The Damaru (An hour-glass-shaped drum, held in Shiva's hand.) and horn have to be sounded, drums are to be beaten so as to raise the deep and martial notes, and with "Mahavira, Mahavira" on your lips and shouting "Hara, Hara, Vyom, Vyom" , the quarters are to be reverberated. The music which awakens only the softer feelings of man is to be stopped now for some time. Stopping the light tunes such as Kheâl and Tappâ for some time, the people are to be accustomed to hear the Dhrupad music. Through the thunder-roll of the dignified Vedic hymns, life is to be brought back into the country. In everything the austere spirit of heroic manhood is to be revived. In following such an ideal lies the good of the people and the country. If you can build your character after such an ideal, then a thousand others will follow. But take care that you do not swerve an inch from the ideal. Never lose heart. In eating, dressing, or lying, in singing or playing, in enjoyment or disease, always manifest the highest moral courage. Then only will you attain the grace of Mahâshakti, the Divine Mother.

Disciple: Sir, at times I am overcome by low spirits, I don't know how.

Swamiji: Then think like this: "Whose child am I? I associate with him and shall I have such weak-mindedness and lowness of spirits?" Stamping down such weakness of mind and heart, stand up, saying, "I am possessed of heroism — I am possessed of a steady intellect — I am a knower of Brahman, a man of illumination." Be fully conscious of your dignity by remembering, "I am the disciple of such and such who is the companion-in-life of Shri Ramakrishna, the conqueror of lust and wealth." This will produce a good effect. He who has not this pride has no awakening of Brahman within him. Haven't you heard Râmprasâd's song? He used to say, "Whom do I fear in the world, whose sovereign is the Divine Mother!" Keep such a pride always awake in the mind. Then weakness of mind and heart will no longer be able to approach you. Never allow weakness to overtake your mind. Remember Mahavira, remember the Divine Mother! And you will see that all weakness, all cowardice will vanish at once.

Saying these words, Swamiji came downstairs and took his accustomed seat on a cot in the courtyard. Then, addressing the assembled Sannyasins and Brahmacharins, he said, "Here is the unveiled presence of Brahman. Fie upon those who disregarding It set their mind on other things! Ah! here is Brahman as palpable as a fruit in one's palm. Don't you see? Here!"

These words were spoken in such an appealing way, that every one stood motionless like a figure painted on canvas and felt as if he were suddenly drawn into the depth of meditation. . . . After some time that tension of feeling passed and they regained their normal consciousness.

Next, in the course of a walk, Swamiji spoke to the disciple. "Did you see how everybody had become concentrated today? These are all children of Shri Ramakrishna, and on the very uttering of the words, they felt the truth."

Disciple: Sir, not to speak of them, even my heart was overflowing with an unearthly bliss! But now it appears like a vanished dream.

Swamiji: Everything will come in time. Now, go on working. Set yourself to some work for the good of men sunk in ignorance and delusion. You will see that such experiences will come of themselves.

Disciple: I feel nervous to enter into its labyrinths – neither have I the strength. The scriptures also say, "Impenetrable is the path of Karma".

Swamiji: What do you wish to do then?

Disciple: To live and hold discussion with one like you, who has realised the truth of all scriptures and through hearing, thinking, and meditating on the Truth to realise Brahman in this very life. I have no enthusiasm, nor perhaps the strength, for anything else.

Swamiji: If you love that, well, you can go on doing it. And speak about your thoughts and conclusions about the Shastras to others, it will benefit them. So long as there is the body, one cannot live without doing some work or other; therefore one should do such work as is conducive to the good of others. Your own realisations and conclusions about scriptural truths may benefit many a seeker after Truth. Put them into writing which may help many others.

Disciple: First let me realise the Truth, then I shall write. Shri Ramakrishna used to say; "Without the badge of authority, none will listen to you."

Swamiji: There may be many in the world who have got stuck in that stage of spiritual discipline and reasoning through which you are passing, without being able to pass beyond that stage. Your experience and way of thinking, if recorded, may be of benefit to them at least. If you put down in easy language the substance of the discussions which you hold with the Sadhus of this Math, it may help many.

Disciple: Since you wish it, I shall try to do it.

Swamiji: What is the good of that spiritual practice or realisation which does not benefit others, does not conduce to the well-being of people sunk in ignorance and delusion, does not help in rescuing them from the clutches of lust and wealth? Do you think, so long as one Jiva endures in bondage, you will have any liberation? So long as he is not liberated – it may take several lifetimes – you will have to be born to help him, to make him realise Brahman. Every Jiva is part of yourself – which is the rationale of all work for others. As you desire the whole-hearted good of your wife and children, knowing them to be your own, so when a like amount of love and attraction for every Jiva will awaken in you, then I shall know that Brahman is awakening in you, not a moment before. When this feeling of the all-round good of all without respect for caste or colour will awaken in your heart, then I shall know you are advancing towards the ideal.

Disciple: Sir, it is a most tremendous statement that without the salvation of all, there shall be no salvation for an individual! I have never heard of such a wonderful proposition.

Swamiji: There is a class of Vedantists who hold such a view. They say that individual liberation is not the real and perfect form of liberation, but universal and collective liberation is true Mukti. Of course, both merits and defects can be pointed out in that view.

Disciple: According to Vedanta, the state of individualised existence is the root of bondage, and the Infinite Intelligence, through desires and effects of works, appears bound in that limiting condition. When by means of discrimination that limiting condition vanishes and the Jiva is bereft of all adjuncts, then how can there be bondage for the Atman which is of the essence of transcendent Intelligence? He for whom the idea of the Jiva and the world is a persisting reality may think that without the liberation of all he has no liberation. But when the mind becomes bereft of all limiting adjuncts and is merged in Brahman, where is there any differentiation for him? So nothing can operate as a bar to his Mukti.

Swamiji: Yes, what you say is right, and most Vedantins hold that view, which is also flawless. In that view, individual liberation is not barred. But just consider the greatness of his heart who thinks that he will take the whole universe with him to liberation!

Disciple: Sir, it may indicate boldness of heart, but it is not supported by the scriptures.

Swamiji was in an abstracted mood and did not listen to the words. After some time he said: "Day and night think and meditate on Brahman, meditate with great one-pointedness of mind. And during the time of awakeness to outward life, either do some work for the sake of others or repeat in your mind, 'Let good happen to Jivas and the world!' 'Let the mind of all flow in the direction of Brahman!' Even by such continuous current of thought the world will be benefited. Nothing good in the world becomes fruitless, be it work or thought. Your thought-currents will perhaps rouse the religious feeling of someone in America."

Disciple: Sir, please bless me that my mind may be concentrated on the Truth.

Swamiji: So it will be. If you have earnestness of desire, it will certainly be.

XXII

(From the Diary of a Disciple (Shri Sharat Chandra Chakravarty, B.A.))

(Translated from Bengali)

[Place: The Math, Belur. Year: 1901.]

At the time Belur Math was established, many among the orthodox Hindus were wont to make sharp criticism of the ways of life in the Math. Hearing the report of such criticism from the disciple, Swamiji would say (in the words of the couplet of Tulasidas), "The elephant passes in the market-place, and a thousand curs begin barking after him; so the Sadhus have no ill-feeling when worldly people slander then." Or again he would say, "Without persecution no beneficent idea can enter into the heart of a society." He would exhort everybody, "Go on working without an eye to results. One day you are sure to reap the fruits of it." Again, on the lips of Swamiji were very often heard the words of the Gita, "A doer of good never comes to grief, my son."

In May or June, 1901, seeing the disciple at the Math Swamiji said, "Bring me a copy of *Ashtâvimshati-tattva* (Twenty-eight Categories) of Raghunandan at an early date."

Disciple: Yes, sir, but what will you do with the Raghunandan Smriti, which the present educated India calls a heap of superstition?

Swamiji: Why? Raghunandan was a wonderful scholar of his time. Collecting the ancient Smritis, he codified the customs and observances of the Hindus, adapting them to the needs of the changed times and circumstances. All Bengal is following the rules laid down by him. But in the iron grip of his rules regulating the life of a Hindu from conception to death, the Hindu society was much oppressed. In matters of eating and sleeping, in even the ordinary functions of life, not to speak of the important ones, he tried to regulate every one by rules. In the altered circumstances of the times, that did not last long. At all times in all countries the Karma-kânda, comprising the social customs and observances, changes form. Only the Jnâna-kânda endures. Even in the Vedic age you find that the rituals gradually changed in form. But the philosophic portion of the Upanishads has remained unchanged up till now — only there have been many interpreters, that is all.

Disciple: What will do you with the Smriti of Raghunandan?

Swamiji: This time I have a desire to celebrate the Durgâ Puja (worship of goddess Durga). If the expenses are forthcoming, I shall worship the Mahâmâyâ. Therefore I have a mind to read the ceremonial forms of that worship. When you come to the Math next Sunday, you must bring a copy of the book with you.

Disciple: All right, sir.

Next Saturday the disciple brought a copy of the book, and Swamiji was much pleased to get it. Meeting the disciple a week after this he said, "I have finished the Raghunandan Smriti presented by you. If possible, I shall celebrate the Puja of the Divine Mother."

* * *

The Durga Puja took place with great *éclat* at the proper time.

Shortly after this Swamiji performed a Homa before the Mother Kali at Kalighat. Referring this incident he spoke to the disciple, "Well, I was glad to see that there was yet a liberality of view at Kalighat. The temple authorities did not object in the least to my entering the temple, though they knew that I was a man who had returned from the West. On the contrary, they very cordially took me into the holy precincts and helped me to worship the Mother to my heart's content."

XXIII

(From the Diary of a Disciple (Shri Sharat Chandra Chakravarty, B.A.))

(Translated from Bengali)

[Place: The Math, Belur. Year: 1902.]

Today is the anniversary celebration of Shri Ramakrishna – the last that Swamiji ever saw. The disciple presented an invocatory hymn on Shri Ramakrishna to Swamiji. He then proceeded to rub Swamiji's feet gently. Before starting to read the poem, Swamiji spoke to him: "Do it very gently as the feet have become very tender."

After reading the poem Swamiji said, "It is well done."

Swamiji's illness had increased so much that the disciple, observing it, felt sore at heart. Understanding his inner feeling, Swamiji said, "What are you thinking? This body is born and it will die. If I have been able to instil a few of my ideas into you all, then I shall know that my birth has not been in vain."

Disciple: Are we fit objects of your mercy? If you bless me, without taking my fitness into consideration, then I will consider myself fortunate.

Swamiji: Always remember that renunciation is the root idea. Unless one is initiated into this idea, not even Brahmâ and the World-Gods have the power to attain Mukti.

Disciple: It is a matter of deep regret that even hearing this from you almost every day, I have not been able to realise it.

Swamiji: Renunciation must come, but in the fulness of time. " – In the fulness of time one attains to knowledge within himself." When the few Samskâras (tendencies) of the previous life are spent, then renunciation sprouts up in the heart.

After some time he said, "Why should you go outside and see the big concourse of people? Stay with me now. And ask Niranjan to sit at the door, so that nobody may disturb me today."

Then the following conversation took place between Swamiji and the disciple:

Swamiji: I think that it will be better if from now the anniversary is celebrated in a different way. The celebration should extend to four or five days instead of one. On the first day, there may be study and interpretation of scriptures; on the second, discussion on the Vedas and the Vedanta and the solution of the problems in connection with them; on the third day, there may be a question class. The fourth day may be fixed for lectures. On the last day, there will be a festival on the present lines. This will be like the Durga Puja extending over four or five days. Of course, if the celebration is on the above lines, none but the devotees of Shri Ramakrishna will be able to attend on the other days except the last. But that does not matter. A large promiscuous crowd of people does not mean a great propagation of the message of Shri Ramakrishna.

Disciple: Sir, it is a beautiful idea. Next time it will be done according to your wishes.

Swamiji: Now, my son, you all will carry them out. I have no more inclination for these things.

Disciple: Sir, this year many Kirtana parties have come.

Hearing these words Swamiji stood up holding the iron bars of the window and looked at the assembled crowd of devotees. After some time he sat down.

Swamiji: You are the actors in the Divine Lilâ (play) of Shri Ramakrishna. After this, not to speak of ours, people will take your names also. These hymns which you are writing will afterwards be read by people for the acquirement of love and knowledge. Know that the attainment of the knowledge of the Atman is the highest object of life. If you have devotion for the Avataras who are the world-teachers, that knowledge will manifest of itself in time.

Disciple: Sir, shall I attain to such knowledge?

Swamiji: By the blessings of Shri Ramakrishna you shall attain to divine love and knowledge. You will not find much happiness in the worldly life.

Disciple: Sir, if you condescend to destroy the weakness of my mind, then only there is hope for me.

Swamiji: What fear! When you have chanced to come here, you shall be free.

Disciple (with great entreaty): You must save me and lift me from ignorance in this very life.

Swamiji: Say, who can save anybody? The Guru can only take away some covering veils. When these veils are removed, the Atman shines in Its own glory and manifests like the sun.

Disciple: Then why do we find mention of grace in the scriptures?

Swamiji: Grace means this. He who has realised the Atman becomes a storehouse of great power. Making him the centre and with a certain radius a circle is formed, and whoever comes within the circle becomes animated with the ideas of that saint, i.e. they are overwhelmed by his ideas. Thus without much religious striving, they inherit the results of his wonderful spirituality. If you call this grace, you may do so.

Disciple: Is there no other grace than this?

Swamiji: Yes, there is. When the Avatara comes, then with him are born liberated persons as helpers in his world-play. Only Avataras have the power to dispel the darkness of a million souls and give them salvation in one life. This is known as grace. Do you understand?

Disciple: Yes, sir. But what is the way for those who have not been blessed with the sight of him?

Swamiji: The way for them is to call on him. Calling on him, many are blessed with his vision – can see him in human form just like ours and obtain his grace.

Disciple: Have you ever had a vision of Shri Ramakrishna after his passing away?

Swamiji: After his leaving the body, I associated for some time with Pavhâri Bâbâ of Ghazipur. There was a garden not far distant from his Âshrama where I lived. People used to say it was a haunted garden, but as you know, I am a sort of demon myself and have not much fear of ghosts. In the garden there were many lemon trees which bore numerous fruits. At that time I was suffering from diarrhoea, and there no food could be had except bread. So, to increase the digestive powers, I used to take plenty of lemons. Mixing with Pavhari Baba, I liked him very much, and he also came to love me deeply. One day I thought that I did not learn any art for making this weak body strong, even though I lived with Shri Ramakrishna for so many years. I had heard that Pavhari Baba knew the science of Hatha-Yoga. So I thought I would learn the practices of Hatha-Yoga from him, and through them strengthen the body. You know, I have a dogged resolution, and whatever I set my heart on, I always carry out. On the eve of the day on which I was to take initiation, I was lying on a cot thinking; and just then I saw the form of Sri Ramakrishna standing on my right side, looking steadfastly at me, as if very much grieved. I had dedicated myself to him, and at the thought that I was taking another Guru I was much ashamed and kept looking at him. Thus perhaps two or three hours passed, but no words escaped from my mouth. Then he disappeared all on a sudden. My mind became upset seeing Shri Ramakrishna that night, so I postponed the idea of initiation from Pavhari Baba for the day. After a day or two again the idea of initiation from Pavhari Baba arose in the mind – and again in the night there was the appearance of Shri Ramakrishna as on the previous occasion. Thus when for several nights in succession I had the vision of Shri Ramakrishna, I gave up the idea of initiation altogether, thinking that as every time I resolved on it, I was getting such a vision, then no good but harm would come from it.

After some time he addressed the disciple, saying, "Those who have seen Shri Ramakrishna are really blessed. Their family and birth have become purified by it. All of you will also get his vision. The very fact that you have come here, shows that you are very near to him. Nobody has been able to understand who came on earth as Sri Ramakrishna. Even his own nearest devotees have got no real clue to it. Only some have got a little inkling of it. All will understand it afterwards."

The conversation was thus going on when Swami Niranjanananda knocked at the door. The disciple rose and inquired, "Who has come?" Swami Niranjanananda replied, "Sister Nivedita and some other English ladies." They were admitted into the room, sat on the floor and inquired about the health of Swamiji. After a few more words they went away. Then Swamiji said to the disciple, "See how cultured they are! If they were Bengalis, they would have made me talk at least for half an hour, even though they found me unwell."

It is about half past two now, and there is a great gathering of people outside. Understanding the disciple's mind, Swamiji said, "Just go and have a look round – but come back soon."

XXIV

(From the Diary of a Disciple (Shri Sharat Chandra Chakravarty, B.A.))

(Translated from Bengali)

[Place: The Math, Belur. Year: 1902.]

After returning from Eastern Bengal Swamiji stayed in the Math and lived a simple childlike life. Every year some Santal labourers used to work in the Math. Swamiji would joke and make fun with them and loved to hear their tales of weal and woe. One day several noted gentlemen of Calcutta came to visit Swamiji in the Math. That day Swamiji had started such a warm talk with the Santals that, when he was informed of the arrival of those gentlemen, he said, "I shan't be able to go now. I am happy with these men." Really that day Swamiji did not leave the poor Santals to see those visitors.

One among the Santals was named Keshta. Swamiji loved Keshta very much. Whenever Swamiji came to talk with them, Keshta used to say to Swamiji, "O my Swamiji, do not come to us when we are working, for while talking with you our work stops and the supervising Swami rebukes us afterwards." Swamiji would be touched by these words and say, "No, no, he will not say anything; tell me a little about your part of the country" — saying which he used to introduce the topic of their worldly affairs.

One day Swamiji said to Keshta, "Well, will you take food here one day?" Keshta said, "We do not take food touched by you; if you put salt in our food and we eat it, we shall lose our caste." Swamiji said, "Why should you take salt? We will prepare curry for you without salt, will you then take it?" Keshta agreed to it. Then at orders of Swamiji, bread, curry, sweets, curd, etc. were arranged for the Santals, and he made them sit before him to eat. While eating, Keshta said, "Whence have you got such a thing? We never tasted anything like this." Feeding them sumptuously, Swamiji said, "You are Nârâyanas, God manifest; today I have offered food to Narayana."

The service of "Daridra Narayana" – God in the poor – about which Swamiji spoke, he himself performed one day like this.

After their meal, the Santals went for rest, and Swamiji, addressing the disciple, said, "I found them the veritable embodiment of God – such simplicity, such sincere guileless love I have seen nowhere else." Then, addressing the Sannyasins of the Math, he said, "See how simple they are. Can you mitigate their misery a little? Otherwise, of what good is the wearing of the Gerua robe? Sacrifice of everything for the good of others is real Sannyasa. They have never enjoyed any good thing in life. Sometimes I feel a desire to sell the Math and everything, and distribute the money to the poor and destitute. We have made the tree our shelter. Alas! the people of the country cannot get anything to eat, and how can we have the heart to raise food to our mouths? When I was in the Western countries, I prayed to the Divine Mother, "People here are sleeping on a bed of flowers, they eat all kinds of delicacies, and what do they not enjoy, while people in our country are dying of starvation. Mother, will there be no way for them! One of the objects of my going to the West to preach religion was to see if I could find any means for feeding the people of this country.

"Seeing the poor people of our country starving for food, a desire comes to me to overthrow all ceremonial worship and learning, and go round from village to village collecting money from the rich by convincing them through force of character and Sadhana, and to spend the whole life in serving the poor.

"Alas! nobody thinks of the poor of this land. They are the backbone of the country, who by their labour are producing food-these poor people, the sweepers and labourers, who if they stop work for one day will create a panic in the town. But there is none to sympathise with them, none to console them in their misery. Just see, for want of sympathy from the Hindus, thousands of Pariahs in Madras are turning Christians. Don't think this is simply due to the pinch of hunger; it is because they do not get any sympathy from us. We are day and night calling out to them, 'Don't touch us! Don't touch us!' Is there any compassion or kindliness of heart in the country? Only a class of 'Don't-touchists'; kick such customs out! I sometimes feel the urge to break the barriers of 'Don't-touchism', to go at once and call out, 'Come, all who are poor, miserable, wretched, and down-trodden', and to bring them all together in the name of Shri Ramakrishna. Unless they rise, the Mother won't awaken. We could not make any provision for food and clothes for these – what have we done then? Alas! they know nothing of worldliness, and therefore even after working day and night cannot provide themselves with food and clothes. Let us open their eyes. I see clear as daylight that there is the one Brahman in all, in them and in me — one Shakti dwells in all. The only difference is of manifestation. Unless the blood circulates over the whole body, has any country risen at any time? If one limb is paralysed, then even with the other limbs whole, not much can be done with that body — know this for certain."

Disciple: Sir, there is such a diversity of religions and ideas among the people of this country that it is a difficult affair to bring harmony among them.

Swamiji (in anger): If you think any work difficult, then do not come here. Through the grace of God all paths become easy. Your work is to serve the poor and miserable, without any distinction of caste or colour, and you have no need to think about the results. Your duty is to go on working, and then everything will follow of itself. My method of work is to construct and not to pull down. Read the history of the world, and you will find that a great soul stood as the central figure in a certain period of a country. Animated by his ideas, hundreds of people did good to the world. You are all intelligent boys, and have been coming here for a long time. Say, what have you done? Couldn't you give one life for the service of others? In the next life you may read Vedanta and other philosophies. Give this life for the service of others, then I shall know that your coming here has not been in vain.

Saying these words, Swamiji sat silent, wrapt in deep thought. After some time, he added, "After so much austerity, I have understood this as the real truth — God is present in every Jiva; there is no other God besides that. 'Who serves Jiva, serves God indeed'." After some pause Swamiji, addressing the disciple, said, "What I have told you today, inscribe in your heart. See that you do not forget it."

XXV

(From the Diary of a Disciple (Shri Sharat Chandra Chakravarty, B.A.))

(Translated from Bengali)

[Place: The Math, Belur. Year: beginning of 1902.]

It was Saturday, and the disciple came to the Math just before evening. An austere routine was being followed now at the Math regarding spiritual practices. Swamiji had issued an order that all Brahmacharins and Sannyasins should get up very early in the morning and practise Japa and meditation in the worship-room. Swamiji was having little sleep during these days, and would rise from bed at three in the morning.

On the disciple saluting Swamiji just after his appearance at the Math, he said, "Well, see how they are practising religious exercises here nowadays. Everyone passes a considerable time in Japa and meditation on mornings and evenings. Look there — a bell has been procured, which is used for rousing all from sleep. Everyone has to get up before dawn. Shri Ramakrishna used to say, 'In the morning and evening the mind remains highly imbued with Sattva ideas; those are the times when one should meditate with earnestness.'

"After the passing away of Shri Ramakrishna we underwent a lot of religious practice at the Baranagore Math. We used to get up at 3 a.m. and after washing our face etc.— some after bath, and others without it — we would sit in the worship-room and become absorbed in Japa and meditation. What a strong spirit of dispassion we had in those days! We had no thought even as to whether the world existed or not. Ramakrishnananda busied himself day and night with the duties pertaining to Shri Ramakrishna's worship and service, and occupied the same position in the Math as the mistress of the house does in a family. It was he who would procure, mostly by begging, the requisite articles for Shri Ramakrishna's worship and our subsistence. There have been days when the Japa and meditation continued from morning till four or five in the afternoon. Ramakrishnananda waited and waited with our meals ready, till at last he would come and snatch us from our meditation by sheer force. Oh, what a wonderful constancy of devotion we have noticed in him!"

Disciple: Sir, how did you use to meet the Math expenses then?

Swamiji: What a question! Well, we were Sadhus, and what would come by begging and other means, would be utilised for defraying the Math expenses. Today both Suresh Babu (Surendra Nath Mitra) and Balaram Babu are no more; had they been alive they would have been exceedingly glad to see this Math. You have doubtless heard Suresh Babu's name. It was he who used to bear all the expenses of the Baranagore Math. It was this Suresh Mitra who used to think most for us in those days. His devotion and faith have no parallel!

Disciple; Sir, I have heard that you did not see him very often while he was dying.

Swamiji: We could only do so if we were allowed (by his relatives). Well, it is a long tale. But know this for certain that among worldly people it is of little count to your relatives and kinsmen whether you live or die. If you succeed in leaving some property, you will find even in your lifetime that there has been set up a brawl over it in your household. You will have no one to console you in your death-bed – not even your wife and sons! Such is the way of the world!

Referring to the past condition of the Math, Swamiji went on, "Owing to want of funds I would sometimes fight for abolishing the Math altogether. But I could never induce Ramakrishnananda to accede to the proposal. Know Ramakrishnananda to be the central figure of the Math. There have been days when the Math was without a grain of food. If some rice was collected by begging, there was no salt to take it with! On some days there would be only rice and salt, but nobody cared for it in the least. We were then being carried away by a tidal wave of spiritual practice. Boiled Bimba leaves, rice, and salt – this was the menu for a month at a stretch. Oh, those wonderful days! The austerities of that period were enough to dismay supernatural beings, not to speak of men. But it is a tremendous truth that if there be real worth in you, the more are circumstances against you, the more will that inner power manifest itself. But the reason why I have provided for beds and a tolerable living in this Math is that the Sannyasins that are enrolling themselves nowadays will not be able to bear so much strain as we did. There was the life of Shri Ramakrishna before us, and that was why we did not care much for privations and hardships. Boys of this generation will not be able to undergo so much hardship. Hence it is that I have provided for some sort of habitation and a bare subsistence for them. If they get just enough food and clothing, the boys will devote themselves to religio practice and will learn to sacrifice their lives for the good of humanity."

Disciple: Sir, outside people say a good deal against this sort of beddi and furniture.

Swamiji: Let them say. Even in jest they will at least once think of t Math. And they say, it is easier to attain liberation through cherishing hostile spirit. Shri Ramakrishna used to say, "Men should be ignored li worms." Do you mean we have to conduct ourselves according to the chan opinion of others? Pshaw!

Disciple: Sir, you sometimes say, "All are Nârâyanas, the poor and t needy are my Narayanas", and again you say, "Men should be ignored li worms." What do you really mean?

Swamiji: Well, there is not the least doubt that all are Narayana But all Narayanas do not criticise the furniture of the Math. I shall go working for the good of men, without caring in the least for the criticis of others — it is in this sense that the expression, "Men are to be ignor like worms", has been used. He who has a dogged determination like th shall have everything. Only some may have it sooner, and others a lit later, that is all. But one is bound to reach the goal. It is because we had su a determination that we have attained the little that we have. Otherwi what dire days of privation we have had to pass through! One day, for wa of food I fainted in the outer platform of a house on the roadside and qu a shower of rain had passed over my head before I recovered my sens Another day, I had to do odd jobs in Calcutta for the whole day witho food, and had my meal on my return to the Math at ten or eleven in t night. And these were not solitary instances.

Saying these words, Swamiji sat for a while pursuing some trend thought. Then he resumed:

Real monasticism is not easy to attain. There is no order of life rigorous as this. If you stumble ever so little, you are hurled down a precip — and are smashed to pieces. One day I was travelling on foot from Ag to Vrindaban. There was not a farthing with me. I was about a couple miles from Vrindaban when I found a man smoking on the roadside, an was seized with a desire to smoke. I said to the man, "Hallo, will you let have a puff at your Chillum?" He seemed to be hesitating greatly and sa "Sire, I am a sweeper." Well, there was the influence of old Samskaras, a I immediately stepped back and resumed my journey without smoking had gone a short distance when the thought occurred to me that I wa Sannyasin, who had renounced caste, family, prestige, and everything and still I drew back as soon as the man gave himself out as a sweeper, a could not smoke at the Chillum touched by him! The thought made me restless at heart; then I had walked on half a mile. Again I retraced my steps and came to the sweeper whom I found still sitting there. I hastened to tell him, "Do prepare a Chillum of tobacco for me, my dear friend." I paid no heed to his objections and insisted on having it. So the man was compelled to prepare a Chillum for me. Then I gladly had a puff at it and proceeded to Vrindaban. When one has embraced the monastic life, one has to test whether one has gone beyond the prestige of caste and birth, etc. It is so difficult to observe the monastic vow in right earnest! There must not be the slightest divergence between one's words and actions.

Disciple: Sir, you sometimes hold before us the householder's ideal and sometimes the ideal of the Sannyasin. Which one are we to adopt?

Swamiji: Well, go on listening to all. Then stick to that one which appeals to you — grip it hard like a bulldog.

Swamiji came downstairs accompanied by the disciple, while speaking these words, and began to pace to and fro, uttering now and then the name of Shiva or humming a song on the Divine Mother, such as, "Who knows how diversely Thou playest, O Mother, Thou flowing stream of nectar", and so on.

XXVI

(From the Diary of a Disciple (Shri Sharat Chandra Chakravarty, B.A.))

(Translated from Bengali)

[Place: The Math, Belur. Year: *1902*.]

The disciple passed the preceding night in Swamiji's room. At 4 a.m. Swamiji roused him and said "Go and knock up the Sadhus and Brahmacharins from sleep with the bell." In pursuance of the order, the disciple rang the bell near the Sadhus who slept. The monastic inmates hastened to go to the worship-room for meditation.

According to Swamiji's instructions, the disciple rang the bell lustily near Swami Brahmananda's bed, which made the latter exclaim, "Good heavens! The Bângâl (Meaning an East Bengal man, used as a term of endearing reproach for the disciple.) has made it too hot for us to stay in the Math!" On the disciple's communicating this to Swamiji, he burst out into a hearty laugh, saying, "Well done!"

Then Swamiji, too, washed his face and entered the chapel accompanied by the disciple.

The Sannyasins — Swami Brahmananda and others — were already seated for meditation. A separate seat was kept for Swamiji, on which he sat facing the east, and pointing to a seat in front to the disciple, said, "Go and meditate, sitting there."

Shortly after taking his seat, Swamiji became perfectly calm and motionless, like a statue, and his breathing became very slow. Everyone else kept his seat.

After about an hour and a half, Swamiji rose from meditation with the words "Shiva, Shiva". His eyes were flushed, the expression placid, calm, and grave. Bowing before Shri Ramakrishna he came downstairs and paced the courtyard of the Math. After a while he said to the disciple. "Do you see how the Sadhus are practising meditation etc. nowadays? When the meditation is deep, one sees many wonderful things. While meditating at the Baranagore Math, one day I saw the nerves Idâ and Pingalâ. One can see them with a little effort. Then, when one has a vision of the Shushumnâ, one can see anything one likes. If a man has unflinching devotion to the Guru, spiritual practices — meditation, Japa, and so forth — come quite naturally; one need not struggle for them. 'The Guru is Brahmâ, the Guru is Vishnu, and the Guru is Shiva Himself.'"

Then the disciple prepared tobacco for Swamiji and when he returned with it, Swamiji spoke as he puffed at it, "Within there is the lion — the eternally pure, illumined, and ever free Atman; and directly one realises Him through meditation and concentration, this world of Maya vanishes. He is equally present in all; and the more one practises, the quicker does the Kundalini (the 'coiled-up' power) awaken in him. When this power reaches the head, one's vision is unobstructed — one realises the Atman."

Disciple: Sir, I have only read of these things in the scriptures, but nothing has been realised as yet.

Swamiji: कालेनात्मनि विन्दति — is bound to come in time. But some attain this early, and others are a little late. One must stick to it — determined never to let it go. This is true manliness. You must keep the mind fixed on one object, like an unbroken stream of oil. The ordinary man's mind is scattered on different objects, and at the time of meditation, too, the mind is at first apt to wander. But let any desire whatever arise in the mind, you must sit calmly and watch what sort of ideas are coming. By continuing to watch in that way, the mind becomes calm, and there are no more thought-waves in it. These waves represent the thought-activity of the mind. Those things that you have previously thought deeply, have transformed themselves into a subconscious current, and therefore these come up in the mind in meditation. The rise of these waves, or thoughts, during meditation is an evidence that your mind is tending towards concentration. Sometimes the mind is concentrated on a set of ideas — this is called meditation with Vikalpa or oscillation. But when the mind becomes almost free from all activities, it melts in the inner Self, which is the essence of infinite Knowledge, One, and Itself Its own support. This is what is called Nirvikalpa Samâdhi, free from all activities. In Shri Ramakrishna we have again and again noticed both these forms of Samadhi. He had not to struggle to get these states. They came to him spontaneously, then and there. It was a wonderful phenomenon. It was by seeing him that we could rightly understand these things. Meditate every day alone. Everything will open up of itself. Now the Divine Mother — the embodiment of illumination — is sleeping within, hence you do not understand this. She is the Kundalini. When, before meditating, you proceed to "purify the nerves", you must mentally strike hard on the Kundalini in the Mulâdhâra (sacral plexus), and repeat, "Arise, Mother, arise!" One must practise these slowly. During meditation, suppress the emotional side altogether. This is a great source of danger. Those that are very emotional no doubt have their Kundalini rushing quickly upwards, but it is as quick to come down as to go up. And when it does come down, it leaves the devotee in a state of utter ruin. It is for this reason that Kirtanas and other auxiliaries to emotional development have a great drawback. It is true that by dancing and jumping, etc. through a momentary impulse, that power is made to course upwards, but it is never enduring. On the contrary when it traces back its course, it rouses violent lust in the individual. Listening to my lectures in America, through temporary excitement many among the audience used to get into an ecstatic state, and some would even become motionless like statues. But on inquiry I afterwards found that many of them had an excess of the carnal instinct immediately after that state. But this happens simply owing to a lack of steady practice in meditation and concentration.

Disciple: Sir, in no scriptures have I ever read these secrets of spiritual practice. Today I have heard quite new things.

Swamiji: Do you think the scriptures contain all the secrets of spiritual practice? These are being handed down secretly through a succession of Gurus and disciples. Practise meditation and concentration with the utmost care. Place fragrant flowers in front and burn incense. At the outset take such external help as will make the mind pure. As you repeat the name of your Guru and Ishta, say, "Peace be to all creatures and the universe!" First send impulses of these good wishes to the north, south, east, west, above, below – in all directions, and then sit down to meditate. One has to do this during the early stages. Then sitting still (you may face in any direction), meditate in the way I have taught you while initiating. Don't leave out a single day. If you have too much pressing work, go through the spiritual exercises for at least a quarter of an hour. Can you reach the goal without steadfast devotion, my son?

Now Swamiji went upstairs, and as he did so, he said, "You people will have your spiritual insight opened without much trouble. Now that you have chanced to come here, you have liberation and all under your thumb. Besides practising meditation, etc., set yourselves heart and soul to remove to a certain extent the miseries of the world, so full of wails. Through hard austerities I have almost ruined this body. There is hardly any energy left in this pack of bones and flesh. You set yourselves to work now, and let me rest a while. If you fail to do anything else, well, you can tell the world at large about the scriptural truths you have studied so long. There is no higher gift than this, for the gift of knowledge is the highest gift in the world."

XXVII

(From the Diary of a Disciple (Shri Sharat Chandra Chakravarty, B.A.))

(Translated from Bengali)

[Place: The Math, Belur. Year: *1902.]*

Swamiji was now staying at the Math. The disciple came to the Math and towards the evening accompanied Swamiji and Swami Premananda for a walk. Finding Swamiji absorbed in thought, the disciple entered into a conversation with Swami Premananda on what Shri Ramakrishna used to say of Swamiji's greatness. After walking some distance Swamiji turned to go back to the Math. Seeing Swami Premananda and the disciple near by, he said, "Well, what were you talking?" The disciple said, "We were talking about Shri Ramakrishna and his words." Swamiji only heard the reply, but again lapsed into thought and walking along the road returned to the Math. He sat on the camp-cot placed under the mango-tree and, resting there some time, washed his face and then, pacing the upper verandah, spoke to the disciple thus: "Why do you not set about propagating Vedanta in your part of the country? There Tântrikism prevails to a fearful extent. Rouse and agitate the country with the lion-roar of Advaitavâda (monism). Then I shall know you to be a Vedantist. First open a Sanskrit school there and teach the Upanishads and the *Brahma-Sutras*. Teach the boys the system of Brahmacharya. I have heard that in your country there is much logic-chopping of the Nyâya school. What is there in it? Only Vyâpti (pervasiveness) and Anumâna (inference) – on these subjects the Pandits of the Nyaya school discuss for months! What does it help towards the Knowledge of the Atman? Either in your village or Nag Mahashaya's, open a Chatushpâthi (indigenous school) in which the scriptures will be studied and also the life and teachings of Shri Ramakrishna. In this way you will advance your own good as well as the good of the people, and your fame will endure.

Disciple: Sir, I cherish no desire for name or fame. Only, sometimes I feel to do as you are saying. But by marriage I have got so entangled in the world that I fear my desire will always remain in the mind only.

Swamiji: What if you have married? As you are maintaining your parents and brothers with food and clothing, so do for your wife likewise; and by giving her religious instruction draw her to your path. Think her to be a partner and helper in the living of your religious life. At other times look upon her with an even eye with others. Thinking thus all the unsteadiness of the mind will die out. What fear?

The disciple felt assured by these words. After his meal, Swamiji sat on his own bed, and the disciple had an opportunity of doing some personal service for him.

Swamiji began to speak to the disciple, enjoining him to be reverential to the Math members: "These children of Shri Ramakrishna whom you see, are wonderful Tyâgis (selfless souls), and by service to them you will attain to the purification of mind and be blessed with the vision of the Atman. You remember the words of the Gita: 'By interrogation and service to the great soul'. Therefore you must serve them, by which you will attain your goal; and you know how much they love you."

Disciple: But I find it very difficult to understand them. Each one seems to be of a different type.

Swamiji: Shri Ramakrishna was a wonderful gardener. Therefore he has made a bouquet of different flowers and formed his Order. All different types and ideas have come into it, and many more will come. Shri Ramakrishna used to say, "Whoever has prayed to God sincerely for one day, must come here." Know each of those who are here to be of great spiritual power. Because they remain shrivelled before me, do not think them to be ordinary souls. When they will go out, they will be the cause of the awakening of spirituality in people. Know them to be part of the spiritual body of Shri Ramakrishna, who was the embodiment of infinite religious ideas. I look upon them with that eye. See, for instance, Brahmananda, who is here — even I have not the spirituality which he has. Shri Ramakrishna looked upon him as his mind-born son; and he lived and walked, ate and slept with him. He is the ornament of our Math — our king. Similarly Premananda, Turiyananda, Trigunatitananda, Akhandananda, Saradananda, Ramakrishnananda, Subodhananda, and others; you may go round the world, but it is doubtful if you will find men of such spirituality and faith in God like them. They are each a centre of religious power, and in time that power will manifest.

The disciple listened in wonder, and Swamiji said again: "But from your part of the country, except Nag Mahashaya none came to Shri Ramakrishna. A few others who saw Shri Ramakrishna could not appreciate him." At the thought of Nag Mahashaya, Swamiji kept silent for some time. It was only four or five months since he had passed away. Swamiji had heard that on one occasion a spring of Ganga water rose in the house of Nag Mahashaya, and recollecting this he asked the disciple, "Well, how did that event take place? Tell me about it."

Disciple: I only heard about it, but did not see it with my own eyes. I heard that in a Mahâvâruni Yoga Nag Mahashaya started with his father for Calcutta. But not getting any accommodation in the railway train he stayed for three or four days in Narayangunge in vain and returned home. Then Nag Mahashaya said to his father, "If the mind is pure, then the Mother Ganga will appear here." Then at the auspicious hour of the holy bath, a jet of water rose, piercing the ground of his courtyard. Many of those who saw it are living today. But that was many years before I met him.

Swamiji: There was nothing strange in it. He was a saint of unfalsified determination. I do not consider such a phenomenon at all strange in his case.

Saying this, Swamiji, feeling sleepy, lay on his side. At this the disciple came down to take his supper.

XXVIII

(From the Diary of a Disciple (Shri Sharat Chandra Chakravarty, B.A.))

(Translated from Bengali)

[Place: From Calcutta to the Math on a boat. Year: 1902.]

While walking on the banks of the Ganga at Calcutta one afternoc the disciple saw a Sannyasin in the distance approaching towards Ahiritc Ghat. While he came near, the disciple found the Sannyasin to be no oth than his Guru, Swami Vivekananda. In his left hand he had a leaf receptac containing fried gram, which he was eating like a boy, and was walking great joy. When he stood before him, the disciple fell at his feet and ask the reason for his coming to Calcutta unexpectedly.

Swamiji: I came on business. Come, will you go to the Math? Eat a lit of the fried gram. It has a nice saline and pungent taste.

The disciple took the food with gladness and agreed to go to the Ma with him.

Swamiji: Then look for a boat.

The disciple hurried to hire a boat. He was settling the amount of t boat-hire with the boatman, who demanded eight annas, when Swan also appeared on the scene and stopped the disciple saying, "Why are y higgling with them?" and said to the boatman, "Very well, I will give y eight annas", and got into the boat. That boat proceeded slowly against t current and took nearly an hour and half to reach the Math. Being alo with Swamiji in the boat, the disciple had an opportunity of asking h freely about all subjects. Raising the topic of the glorificatory poem whi the disciple had recently composed singing the greatness of the devote of Shri Ramakrishna, Swamiji asked him, "How do you know that the whom you have named in your hymn are the near and intimate disciples Shri Ramakrishna?"

Disciple: Sir, I have associated with the Sannyasin and householder disciples of Shri Ramakrishna for so many years; I have heard from them that they are all devotees of Shri Ramakrishna.

Swamiji: Yes, they are devotees of Shri Ramakrishna. But all devotees do not belong to the group of his most intimate and nearest disciples. Staying in the Cossipore Garden, Shri Ramakrishna said to us, "The Divine Mother showed me that all of these are not my inner devotees." Shri Ramakrishna said so that day with respect to both his men and women devotees.

Then speaking of the way Shri Ramakrishna would indicate different grades among devotees, high and low, Swamiji began to explain to the disciple at length the great difference there is between the householder's and the Sannyasin's life.

Swamiji: Is it possible that one would serve the path of lust and wealth and understand Shri Ramakrishna aright at the same time? Or will it ever be possible? Never put your faith in such words. Many among the devotees of Shri Ramakrishna are now proclaiming themselves as Ishvara-koti (of Divine class), Antaranga (of inner circle), etc. They could not imbibe his great renunciation or dispassion, yet they say they are his intimate devotees! Sweep away all such words. He was a prince of Tyagis (self-renouncers), and obtaining his grace can anybody spend his life in the enjoyment of lust and wealth?

Disciple: Is it then, sir, that those who came to him at Dakshineswar were not his devotees?

Swamiji: Who says that? Everybody who has gone to Shri Ramakrishna has advanced in spirituality, is advancing, and will advance. Shri Ramakrishna used to say that the perfected Rishis of a previous Kalpa (cycle) take human bodies and come on earth with the Avataras. They are the associates of the Lord. God works through them and propagates His religion. Know this for a truth that they alone are the associates of the Avatara who have renounced all self for the sake of others, who, giving up all sense-enjoyments with repugnance, spend their lives for the good of the world, for the welfare of the Jivas. The disciples of Jesus were all Sannyasins. The direct recipients of the grace of Shankara, Ramanuja, Shri Chaitanya and Buddha were the all-renouncing Sannyasins. It is men of this stamp who have been through succession of disciples spreading the

Brahma-vidyâ (knowledge of Brahman) in the world. Where and when have you heard that a man being the slave of lust and wealth has been able to liberate another or to show the path of God to him? Without himself free, how can he make others free? In Veda, Vedanta, Itihâsa (history), Purâna (ancient tradition), you will find everywhere that the Sannyasins have been the teachers of religion in all ages and climes. History repeats itself. It will also be likewise now. The capable Sannyasin children of Shri Ramakrishna, the teacher of the great synthesis of religions, will be honoured everywhere as the teachers of men. The words of others will dissipate in the air like an empty sound. The real self-sacrificing Sannyasins of the Math will be the centre of the preservation and spread of religious ideas. Do you understand?

Disciple: Then is it not true – what the householder devotees of Shri Ramakrishna are preaching about him in diverse ways?

Swamiji: It can't be said that they are altogether false; but what they are saying about Shri Ramakrishna is only partial truth. According to one's own capacity, one has understood Shri Ramakrishna and so is discussing about him. It is not bad either to do so. But if any of his devotees has concluded that what he has understood of him is the only truth, then he is an object of pity. Some are saying that Shri Ramakrishna was a Tantrika and Kaula, some that he was Shri Chaitanya born on earth to preach "Nâradiya Bhakti" (Bhakti as taught by Nâradâ); some again that to undertake spiritual practices is opposed to faith in him as an Avatara while some are opining that it is not agreeable to his teachings to take to Sannyasa. You will hear such words from the householder devotees, but do not listen to such one-sided estimates. He was the concentrated embodiment of how many previous Avataras! Even spending the whole life in religious austerity, we could not understand it. Therefore one has to speak about him with caution and restraint. As are one's capacities, so he fills one with spiritual ideas. One spray from the full ocean of his spirituality, if realised, will make gods of men. Such a synthesis of universal ideas you will not find in the history of the world again. Understand from this who was born in the person of Shri Ramakrishna. When he used to instruct his Sannyasin disciples, he would rise from his seat and look about to see if any householder was coming that way or not. If he found none, then in glowing words he would depict the glory of renunciation and austerity. As a result of the rousing power of that fiery dispassion, we have renounced the world and become averse to worldliness.

Disciple: He used to make such distinctions between householders and Sannyasins!

Swamiji: Ask and learn from the householder devotees themselves about it. And you yourself can think and know which are greater – those of his children who for the realisation of God have renounced all enjoyments of the worldly life and are spending themselves in the practice of austerities on hills and forests, Tirthas and Ashramas (holy places and hermitages), or those who are praising and glorifying his name and practising his remembrance, but are not able to rise above the delusion and bondage of the world? Which are greater – those who are coming forward in the service of humanity, regarding them as the Atman, those who are continent since early age, who are the moving embodiments of renunciation and dispassion, or those who like flies are at one time sitting on a flower, and at the next moment on a dung heap? You can yourself think and come to a conclusion.

Disciple: But, sir, what does the world really mean to those who have obtained his grace? Whether they remain in the householder's life or take to Sannyasa, it is immaterial – so it appears to me.

Swamiji: The mind of those who have truly received his grace cannot be attached to worldliness. The test of his grace is-unattachment to lust or wealth. If that has not come in anyone's life, then he has not truly received his grace.

When the above discussion ended thus, the disciple raising another topic, asked Swamiji, "Sir, what is the outcome of all your labours here and in foreign countries?"

Swamiji: You will see only a little manifestation of what has been done. In time the whole world must accept the universal and catholic ideas of Shri Ramakrishna and of this, only the beginning has been made. Before this flood everybody will be swept off.

Disciple: Please tell me more about Shri Ramakrishna. I like very much to hear of him from your lips.

Swamiji: You are hearing so much about him all the time, what more? He himself is his own parallel. Has he any exemplar?

Disciple: What is the way for us who have not seen him?

Swamiji: You have been blessed with the company of these Sadhus who are the direct recipients of his grace. How then can you say you have not seen him? He is present among his Sannyasin disciples. By service to them, he will in time be revealed in your heart. In time you will realise everything.

Disciple: But, sir, you speak about others who have received his grace, but never about what he used to say about yourself.

Swamiji: What shall I say about myself? You see, I must be one of his demons. In his presence even, I would sometimes speak ill of him, hearing which he would laugh.

Saying thus Swamiji's face assumed a grave aspect, and he looked towards the river with an absent mind and sat still for some time. Within a short time the evening fell and the boat also reached the Math. Swamiji was then humming a tune to himself, "Now in the evening of life, take the child back to his home."

When the song was finished, Swamiji said, "In your part of the country (East Bengal) sweet-voiced singers are not born. Without drinking the water of mother Ganga, a sweet, musical voice is not acquired."

After paying the hire, Swamiji descended from the boat and taking off his coat sat in the western verandah of the Math. His fair complexion and ochre robe presented a beautiful sight.

XXIX

(From the Diary of a Disciple (Shri Sharat Chandra Chakravarty, B.A.))

(Translated from Bengali)

[Place: Belur Math. Year: *1902.*]

Today is the first of Âshârh (June-July). The disciple has come to the Math before dusk from Bally, with his office-dress on, as he has not found time to change it. Coming to the Math, he prostrated himself at the feet of Swamiji and inquired about his health. Swamiji replied that he was well, but looking at his dress, he said, "You put on coat and trousers, why don't you put on collars?" Saying this, he called Swami Saradananda who was near and said, "Give him tomorrow two collars from my stock." Swami Saradananda bowed assent to his order.

The disciple then changed his office-dress and came to Swamiji, who, addressing him, said, "By giving up one's national costume and ways of eating and living, one gets denationalised. One can learn from all, but that learning which leads to denationalisation does not help one's uplift but becomes the cause of degradation."

Disciple: Sir, one cannot do without putting on dress approved by superior European officers in official quarters.

Swamiji: No one prevents that. In the interests of your service, you put on official dress in official quarters. But on returning home you should be a regular Bengali Babu – with flowing cloth, a native shirt, and with the Chudder on the shoulder. Do you understand?

Disciple: Yes, sir.

Swamiji: You go about from house to house only with the European shirt on. In the West, to go about visiting people with simply the shirt on is ungentlemanly – one is considered naked. Without putting on a coat over the shirt, you will not be welcomed in a gentleman's house. What nonsense have you learnt to imitate in the matter of dress! Boys and young men nowadays adopt a peculiar manner of dress which is neither Indian nor Western, but a queer combination.

After such talk Swamiji began to pace the bank of the river, and tl disciple was alone with him. He was hesitating to ask Swamiji a questi about religious practices.

Swamiji: What are you thinking? Out with it.

The disciple with great delicacy said, "Sir, I have been thinking that you can teach me some method by which the mind becomes calm withir short time, by which I may be immersed in meditation quickly, I shall fe much benefited. In the round of worldly duties, I feel it difficult to make t mind steady in meditation at the time of spiritual practice."

Swamiji seemed delighted at this humility and earnestness of t disciple. In reply he affectionately said, "After some time come to me wh I am alone upstairs, I will talk to you about it."

Coming up shortly after, the disciple found that Swamiji was sitting meditation, facing the west. His face wore a wonderful expression, and l whole body was completely motionless. The disciple stood by, looking wi speechless wonder on the figure of Swamiji in meditation, and when ev after standing long he found no sign of external consciousness in Swam he sat noiselessly by. After half an hour, Swamiji seemed to show signs o return to external consciousness. The disciple found that his folded han began to quiver, and a few minutes later Swamiji opened his eyes a looking at the disciple said, "When did you come?"

Disciple: A short while ago.

Swamiji: Very well, get me a glass of water.

The disciple hurriedly brought a glass of water and Swamiji drinkin little, asked the disciple to put the glass back in its proper place. The disci did so and again sat by Swamiji.

Swamiji: Today I had a very deep meditation.

Disciple: Sir, please teach me so that my mind also may get absorb in meditation.

Swamiji: I have already told you all the methods. Meditate every d accordingly, and in the fulness of time you will feel like that. Now tell what form of Sadhana appeals to you most.

Disciple: Sir, I practise every day as you have told me, still I do get a deep meditation. Sometimes I think it is useless for me to pract meditation. So I feel that I shall not fare well in it, and therefore now des only eternal companionship with you.

Swamiji: Those are weaknesses of the mind. Always try to get absorb in the eternally present Atman. If you once get the vision of the Atman, y will get everything — the bonds of birth and death will be broken.

Disciple: You bless me to attain to it. You asked me, still I don't get a deep meditation. By some means, do please make my mind steady.

Swamiji: Meditate whenever you get time. If the mind once enters the path of Sushumna, everything will get right. You will not have to do much after that.

Disciple: You encourage me in many ways. But shall I be blessed with a vision of the Truth? Shall I get freedom by attaining true knowledge?

Swamiji: Yes, of course. Everybody will attain Mukti, from a worm up to Brahmâ, and shall you alone fail? These are weaknesses of the mind; never think of such things.

After this, he said again: "Be possessed of Shraddhâ (faith), of Virya (courage), attain to the knowledge of the Atman, and sacrifice your life for the good of others — this is my wish and blessing."

The bell for the meal ringing at this moment, Swamiji asked the disciple to go and partake of it. The disciple, prostrating himself at the feet of Swamiji, prayed for his blessings. Swamiji putting his hand on his head blessed him and said, "If my blessings be of any good to you, I say — may Bhagavân Shri Ramakrishna give you his grace! I know of no blessing higher than this." After meals, the disciple did not go upstairs to Swamiji, who had retired early that night. Next morning the disciple, having to return to Calcutta in the interests of his business appeared before Swamiji upstairs.

Swamiji: Will you go immediately?

Disciple: Yes, sir.

Swamiji: Come again next Sunday, won't you?

Disciple: Yes, certainly.

Swamiji: All right, there is a boat coming.

The disciple took leave of Swamiji. He did not know that this was to be his last meeting with his Ishtadeva (chosen Ideal) in the physical body. Swamiji with a glad heart bade him farewell and said, "Come on Sunday." The disciple replied, "Yes, I will," and got downstairs.

The boatmen were calling for him, so he ran for the boat. Boarding it, he saw Swamiji pacing the upper verandah, and saluting him he entered the boat.

Seven days after this, Swamiji passed away from mortal life. The disciple had no knowledge of the impending catastrophe. Getting the news on the second day of Swamiji's passing away, he came to the Math, and therefore he had not the good fortune to see his physical form again!

XXX

(Translated from Bengali)
[Shri Priya Nath Sinha]

We evince a sad lack of restraint in conversation or any conjoint action such as music and so on. Everyone tries to put himself foremost. The jostling at railway or steamer station is another illustration of his. A friend of Swamiji had a talk with him one day at the Math on this subject. Swamiji remarked, "You see, we have an old adage: 'If your son is not inclined to study, put him in the Durbars (Sâbha).' The word Sabha here does not mean social meetings, such as take place occasionally at people's houses – it means royal Durbars. In the days of the independent kings of Bengal, they used to hold their courts mornings and evenings. There all the affairs of the State were discussed in the morning – and as there were no newspapers at that time, the king used to converse with the leading gentry of the capital and gather from them all information regarding the people and the State. These gentlemen had to attend these meetings, for if they did not do so, the king would inquire into the reason of their non-attendance. Such Durbars were the centres of culture in every country and not merely in ours. In the present day, the western parts of India, especially Rajputana, are much better off in this respect than Bengal, as something similar to these old Durbars still obtains there."

Q. – Then, Maharaj, have our people lost their own good manners because we have no kings of our own?

Swamiji: It is all a degeneration which has its root in selfishness. That in boarding a steamer one follows the vulgar maxim, "Uncle, save thy own precious skin", and in music and moments of recreation everyone tries to make a display of himself, is a typical picture of our mental state. Only a little training in self-sacrifice would take it away. It is the fault of the parents who do not teach their children good manners. Self-sacrifice, indeed, is the basis of all civilisation.

On the other hand, owing to the undue domination exercised by the parents, our boys do not get free scope for growth. The parents consider singing as improper. But the son, when he hears a fine piece of music, at once sets his whole mind on how to learn it, and naturally he must look out for an Âddâ. (Something like a club. The word has got a bad odour about it in Bengali.) Then again, "It is a sin to smoke!" So what else can the young man do than mix with the servants of the house, to indulge in this habit in secret? In everyone there are infinite tendencies, which require proper scope for satisfaction. But in our country that is not allowed; and to bring about a different order of things would require a fresh training of the parents. Such is the condition! What a pity! We have not yet developed a high grade of civilisation; and in spite of this, our educated Babus want the British to hand over the government to them to manage! It makes me laugh and cry as well. Well, where is that martial spirit which, at the very outset, requires one to know how to serve and obey and to practise self-restraint! The martial spirit is not self-assertion but self-sacrifice. One must be ready to advance and lay down one's life at the word of command, before he can command the hearts and lives of others. One must sacrifice himself first.

A devotee of Shri Ramakrishna once passed some severe remarks, in a book written by him, against those who did not believe in Shri Ramakrishna as an Incarnation of God. Swamiji summoned the writer to his presence and addressed him thus in a spirited manner:

What right had you to write like that, abusing others? What matters it if they do not believe in your Lord? Have we created a sect? Are we Ramakrishnites, that we should look upon anyone who will not worship him, as our enemy? By your bigotry you have only lowered him, and made him small. If your Lord is God Himself, then you ought to know that in whatsoever name one is calling upon him, it is *his* worship only — and who are you to abuse others? Do you think they will hear you if you inveigh against them? How foolish! You can only win others' hearts when you have sacrificed yourself to them, otherwise why should they hear you?

Regaining his natural composure after a short while, Swamiji spoke in a sorrowful tone:

Can anyone, my dear friend, have faith or resignation in the Lord, unless he himself is a hero? Never can hatred and malice vanish from one's heart unless one becomes a hero, and unless one is free from these, how can one become truly civilised? Where in this country is that sturdy manliness, that spirit of heroism? Alas, nowhere. Often have I looked for that, and I found only one instance of it, and only one.

Q. — In whom have you found it, Swamiji?

Swamiji: In G. C. (Babu Girish Chandra Ghosh.) alone I have seen that true resignation — that true spirit of a servant of the Lord. And was it not because he was ever ready to sacrifice himself that Shri Ramakrishna took upon himself all his responsibility? What a unique spirit of resignation to the Lord! I have not met his parallel. From him have I learnt the lesson of self-surrender.

So saying, Swamiji raised his folded hands to his head out of respect to him.

XXXI

(Translated from Bengali)

[Shri Priya Nath Sinha]

Arrangements were being made for Swamiji's leaving India for America for the second time (1899 A.D.). He had gone to Calcutta to see one of his friends, and returning from there stopped for a few minutes at Balaram Babu's house at Baghbazar. He then sent for another friend to accompany him to the Math. The friend came, and the following conversation took place between him and Swamiji:

Swamiji: A very funny thing happened today. I went to a friend's house. He has had a picture painted, the subject of which is "Shri Krishna addressing Arjuna on the battlefield of Kurukshetra". Shri Krishna stands on the chariot, holding the reins in His hand and preaching the Gita to Arjuna. He showed me the picture and asked me how I liked it. "Fairly well", I said. But as he insisted on having my criticism on it, I had to give my honest opinion by saying, "There is nothing in it to commend itself to me; first, because the chariot of the time of Shri Krishna was not like the modern pagoda-shaped car, and also, there is no expression in the figure of Shri Krishna."

Q. – Was not the pagoda-chariot in use then?

Swamiji: Don't you know that since the Buddhistic era, there has been a great confusion in everything in our country? The kings never used to fight in pagoda-chariots. There are chariots even today in Rajputana that greatly resemble the chariots of old. Have you seen the chariots in the pictures of Grecian mythology? They have two wheels, and one mounts them from behind; we had that sort of chariot. What good is it to paint a picture if the details are wrong? An historical picture comes up to a standard of excellence when after making proper study and research, things are portrayed exactly as they were at that period. The truth must be represented, otherwise the picture is nothing. In these days, our young men who go in for painting are generally those who were unsuccessful at school, and who have been given up at home as good-for-nothing; what work of art can you expect from them? To paint a really good picture requires as much talent as to produce a perfect drama.

Q. — How then should Shri Krishna be represented in the picture in question?

Swamiji: Shri Krishna ought to be painted as He really was, the Gita personified; and the central idea of the Gita should radiate from His whole form as He was teaching the path of Dharma to Arjuna, who had been overcome by infatuation and cowardice.

So saying Swamiji posed himself in the way in which Shri Krishna should be portrayed, and continued: "Look here, thus does he hold the bridle of the horses — so tight that they are brought to their haunches, with their forelegs fighting the air, and their mouths gaping. This will show a tremendous play of action in the figure of Shri Krishna. His friend, the world-renowned hero, casting aside his bow and arrows, has sunk down like a coward on the chariot, in the midst of the two armies. And Shri Krishna, whip in one hand and tightening the reins with the other, has turned Himself towards Arjuna, with his childlike face beaming with unworldly love and sympathy, and a calm and serene look — and is delivering the message of the Gita to his beloved comrade. Now, tell me what idea this picture of the Preacher of the Gita conveys to you."

The friend: Activity combined with firmness and serenity.

Swamiji: Ay, that's it! Intense action in the whole body, and withal a face expressing the profound calmness and serenity of the blue sky. This is the central idea of the Gita — to be calm and steadfast in all circumstances, with one's body, mind, and soul centred at His hallowed Feet!

कर्मण्यकर्म यः पश्येदकर्मणि च कर्म यः ।
स बुद्धिमान्मनुष्येषु स युक्तः कृत्स्नकर्मकृत् ॥

(Gita IV.18).

He who even while doing action can keep his mind calm, and in whom, even when not doing any outward action, flows the current of activity in the form of the contemplation of Brahman, is the intelligent one among men, he indeed is the Yogi, he indeed is the perfect worker.

At this moment, the man who had been sent to arrange a boat returned and said that it was ready; so Swamiji told his friend, "Now let us go to the Math. You must have left word at home that you were going there with me?"

They continued their talk as they walked to the boat.

Swamiji: This idea must be preached to everyone – work, work, endless work – without looking at results, and always keeping the whole mind and soul steadfast at the lotus feet of the Lord!

Q. – But is this not Karma-Yoga?

Swamiji: Yes, this is Karma-Yoga; but without spiritual practices you will never be able to do this Karma-Yoga. You must harmonise the four different Yogas; otherwise how can you always keep your mind and heart wholly on the Lord?

Q. – It is generally said that work according to the Gita means the performance of Vedic sacrifices and religious exercises; any other kind of work is futile.

Swamiji: All right; but you must make it more comprehensive. Who is responsible for every action you do, every breath you take, and every thought you think? Isn't it you yourself?

The friend: Yes and no. I cannot solve this clearly. The truth about it is that man is the instrument and the Lord is the agent. So when I am directed by His will, I am not at all responsible for my actions.

Swamiji: Well, that can be said only in the highest state of realisation. When the mind will be purified by work and you will *see* that it is He who is causing all to work, then only you will have a right to speak like that. Otherwise it is all bosh, a mere cant.

Q. – Why so, if one is truly convinced by reasoning that the Lord alone is causing all actions to be done?

Swamiji: It may hold good when one *has been so* convinced. But it only lasts for that moment, and not a whit afterwards. Well, consider this thoroughly, whether all that you do in your everyday life, you are not doing with an egoistic idea that you yourself are the agent. How long do you remember that it is the Lord who is making you work? But then, by repeatedly analysing like that, you will come to a state when the ego will vanish and in its place the Lord will come in. Then you will be able to say with justice "Thou, Lord, art guarding all my actions from within." But, my friend, if the ego occupies all the space within your heart, where forsooth will there be room enough for the Lord to come in? The Lord is verily absent!

Q. – But it is He who is giving me the wicked impulse?

Swamiji: No, by no means. It would be blaspheming the Lord to think in that way. He is not inciting you to evil action, it is all the creation of your desire for self-gratification. If one says the Lord is causing everything to be done, and wilfully persists in wrong-doing, it only brings ruin on him.

That is the origin of self-deception. Don't you feel an elation after you ha done a good deed? You then give yourself the credit of doing somethir good – you can't help it, it is very human. But how absurd to take t credit of doing the good act on oneself and lay the blame for the evil act c the Lord! It is a most dangerous idea – the effect of ill-digested Gita ar Vedanta. Never hold that view. Rather say that He is causing the good wo to be done while you are responsible for the evil action. That will bring c devotion and faith, and you will see His grace manifested at every step. T truth about it is that no one has created you – you have created yourse This is discrimination, this is Vedanta. But one does not understand before realisation. Therefore the aspirant should begin with the dualis standpoint, that the Lord is causing the good actions, while he is doing t evil. This is the easiest way to the purification of the mind. Hence you fir dualism so strong among the Vaishnavas. It is very difficult to enterta Advaitic (non-dualistic) ideas at the outset. But the dualistic standpoi gradually leads to the realisation of the Advaita.

Hypocrisy is always a dangerous thing. If there is no wilful se deception, that is to say, if one sincerely believes that the most wick impulse is also prompted by the Lord, rest assured that one will not ha to do those mean acts for long. All the impurities of the mind are quick destroyed. Our ancient scriptural writers understood this well. And I thi that the Tantrika form of worship originated from the time that Buddhis began to decline and, through the oppression of the Buddhists, people beg to perform their Vedic sacrifices in secret. They had no more opportun to conduct them for two months at a stretch, so they made clay imag worshipped them, and consigned them to the water – finishing everythi in one night, without leaving the least trace! Man longs for a concr symbol, otherwise his heart is not satisfied. So in every home that one-nig sacrifice began to take place. As Shri Ramakrishna used to say, "Some en the house by the scavenger's entrance", so the spiritual teachers of that ti saw that those who could not perform any religious rite owing to their e propensities, also needed some way of coming round by degrees to the pa of virtue. For them those queer Tantrika rites came to be invented.

Q. – They went on doing evil actions thinking them to be good. how could this remove their evil tendencies?

Swamiji: Why, they gave a different direction to their propensiti they did them, but with the object of realising the Lord.

Q. – Can this really be done?

Swamiji: It comes to the same thing. The motive must be right. And what should prevent them from succeeding?

Q. – But many are caught in the temptation for wine, meat, etc. in trying to get along with such means.

Swamiji: It was therefore that Shri Ramakrishna came. The days of practising the Tantra in that fashion are gone. He, too, practised the Tantra, but not in that way. Where there is the injunction of drinking wine, he would simply touch his forehead with a drop of it. The Tantrika form of worship is a very slippery ground. Hence I say that this province has had enough of the Tantra. Now it must go beyond. The Vedas should be studied. A harmony of the four kinds of Yogas must be practised and absolute chastity must be preserved.

Q. – What do you mean by the harmony of the four Yogas?

Swamiji: Discrimination between the real and the unreal, dispassion and devotion, work and practices in concentration, and along with these there must be a reverential attitude towards women.

Q. – How can one look with reverence on women?

Swamiji: Well, they are the representatives of the Divine Mother. And real well-being of India will commence from the day that the worship of the Divine Mother will truly begin, and every man will sacrifice himself at the altar of the Mother. . . .

Q. – Swamiji, in your boyhood, when we asked you to marry, you would reply, "I won't, but you will see what I shall become." You have actually verified your words.

Swamiji: Yes, dear brother, you saw how I was in want of food, and had to work hard besides. Oh, the tremendous labour! Today the Americans out of love have given me this nice bed, and I have something to eat also. But, also, I have not been destined to enjoy physically – and lying on the mattress only aggravates my illness. I feel suffocated, as it were. I have to come down and lie on the floor for relief!

XXXII

Vengeance Of History

(Mrs. Wright)

[At the end of August 1893, Swami Vivekananda stayed at Annisquam at the house of Prof. J. H. Wright. So astonishing a sight did Swamiji present in this quiet little New England village that speculations set in at once as to who this majestic and colourful figure might be. From where had he come? At first they decided that he was a Brahmin from India, but his manners did not fully conform to their ideas.] It was something that needed explanation and they unanimously repaired to the cottage after supper, to hear this strange new discourse. . . .

"It was the other day," he said, in his musical voice, "only just the other day – not more than four hundred years ago." And then followed tales of cruelty and oppression, of a patient race and a suffering people, and of a judgment to come! "Ah, the English!" he said. "Only just a little while ago they were savages, the vermin crawled on the ladies' bodies, . . . and they scented themselves to disguise the abominable odour of their persons. . . . Most hor-r-ible! Even now they are barely emerging from barbarism."

"Nonsense," said one of his scandalised hearers, "that was at least five hundred years ago."

"And did I not say 'a little while ago'? What are a few hundred years when you look at the antiquity of the human soul?" Then with a turn of tone, quite reasonable and gentle, "They are quite savage", he said. "The frightful cold, the want and privation of their northern climate", going on more quickly and warmly, "has made them *wild*. They only think to kill. . . . Where is their religion? They take the name of that Holy One, they claim to love their fellowmen, they civilise – by Christianity! – No! It is their hunger that has civilised them, not their God. The love of man is on their lips, in their hearts there is nothing but evil and every violence. 'I love you my brother, I love you!' . . . *and all the while they cut his throat*! Their hands are *red* with blood." . . . Then, going on more slowly, his beautiful voice deepening till it sounded like a bell, "But the judgment of God will fall upon them. 'Vengeance is mine; I will repay, saith the Lord', and destruction is coming. What are your Christians? Not one third of the world. Look at those Chinese, millions of them. They are the vengeance of God that will light upon you. There will be another invasion of the Huns", adding, with a little chuckle, "they will sweep over Europe, they will not leave one stone standing upon another. Men, women, children, all will go and the dark ages will come again." His voice was indescribably sad and pitiful; then suddenly and flippantly, dropping the seer, "Me — I don't care! The world will rise up better from it, but it is coming. The vengeance of God, it is coming soon."

"Soon?" they all asked.

"It will not be a thousand years before it is done."

They drew a breath of relief. It did not seem imminent.

"And God will have vengeance", he went on. "You may not see it in religion, you may not see it in politics, but you must see it in history, and as it has been; it will come to pass. If you grind down the people, you will suffer. We in India are suffering the vengeance of God. Look upon these things. They ground down those poor people for their own wealth, they heard not the voice of distress, they ate from gold and silver when the people cried for bread, and the Mohammedans came upon them slaughtering and killing: slaughtering and killing they overran them. India has been conquered again and again for years, and last and worst of all came the Englishman. You look about India, what has the Hindu left? Wonderful temples, everywhere. What has the Mohammedan left? Beautiful palaces. What has the Englishman left? Nothing but mounds of broken brandy bottles! And God has had no mercy upon my people because they had no mercy. By their cruelty they degraded the populace; and when they needed them, the common people had no strength to give for their aid. If man cannot believe in the Vengeance of God, he certainly cannot deny the Vengeance of History. And it will come upon the English; they have their heels on our necks, they have sucked the last drop of our blood for their own pleasures, they have carried away with them millions of our money, while our people have starved by villages and provinces. And now the Chinaman is the vengeance that will fall upon them; if the Chinese rose today and swept the English into the sea, *as they well deserve*, it would be no more than justice."

And then, having said his say, the Swami was silent. A babble of thin-voiced chatter rose about him, to which he listened, apparently unheeding. Occasionally he cast his eye up to the roof and repeated softly, "Shiva! Shiva!" and the little company, shaken and disturbed by the current of powerful feelings and vindictive passion which seemed to be flowing like molten lava beneath the silent surface of this strange being, broke up, perturbed.

He stayed days [actually it was only a long weekend]. . . . All through, his discourses abounded in picturesque illustrations and beautiful legends. . . .

One beautiful story he told was of a man whose wife reproached him with his troubles, reviled him because of the success of others, and recounted to him all his failures. "Is this what your God has done for you", she said to him, "after you have served Him so many years?" Then the man answered, "Am I a trader in religion? Look at the mountain. What does it do for me, or what have I done for it? And yet I love it because I am so made that I love the beautiful. Thus I love God." . . . There was another story he told of a king who offered a gift to a Rishi. The Rishi refused, but the king insisted and begged that he would come with him. When they came to the palace, he heard the king praying, and the king begged for wealth, for power, for length of days from God. The Rishi listened, wondering, until at last he picked up his mat and started away. Then the king opened his eyes from his prayers and saw him. "Why are you going?" he said. "You have not asked for your gift." "I", said the Rishi, "ask from a beggar?"

When someone suggested to him that Christianity was a saving power, he opened his great dark eyes upon him and said, "If Christianity is a saving power in itself, why has it not saved the Ethiopians, the Abyssinians?"

Often on Swamiji's lips was the phrase, "They would not dare to do this to a monk." . . . At times he even expressed a great longing that the English government would take him and shoot him. "It would be the first nail in their coffin", he would say, with a little gleam of his white teeth. "and my death would run through the land like wild fire."

His great heroine was the dreadful [?] Ranee of the Indian mutiny, who led her troops in person. Most of the old mutineers, he said, had become monks in order to hide themselves, and this accounted very well for the dangerous quality of the monks' opinions. There was one man of them who had lost four sons and could speak of them with composure, but whenever he mentioned the Ranee, he would weep, with tears streaming down his face. "That woman was a goddess", he said, "a *devi*. When overcome, she fell on her sword and died like a man." It was strange to hear the other side of the Indian mutiny, when you would never believe that there was another side to it, and to be assured that a Hindu could not possibly kill a woman . . .

XXXIII

Religion, Civilisation, And Miracles

(The Appeal-Avalanche)

"I am a monk," he said, as he sat in the parlors of La Salette Academy, (On January 21, 1894.) which is his home while in Memphis, "and not a priest. When at home I travel from place to place, teaching the people of the villages and towns through which I pass. I am dependent upon them for my sustenance, as I am not allowed to touch money."

"I was born," he continued, in answer to a question, "in Bengal and become a monk and a celibate from choice. At my birth my father had a horoscope taken of my life, but would never tell me what it was. Some years ago when I visited my home, my father having died, I came across the chart among some papers in my mother's possession and saw from it that I was destined to become a wanderer on the face of the earth."

There was a touch of pathos in the speaker's voice and a murmur of sympathy ran around the group of listeners. Kananda (American reporters generally spelt his name as Vive Kananda in those days.) knocked the ashes from his cigar and was silent for a space.

Presently some one asked:

"If your religion is all that you claim it is, if it is the only true faith, how is it that your people are not more advanced in civilisation than we are? Why has it not elevated them among the nations of the world?"

"Because that is not the sphere of any religion," replied the Hindu gravely. "My people are the most moral in the world, or quite as much as any other race. They are more considerate of their fellow man's rights, and even those of dumb animals, but they are not materialists. No religion has ever advanced the thought or inspiration of a nation or people. In fact, no great achievement has ever been attained in the history of the world that religion has not retarded. Your boasted Christianity has not proven an exception in this respect. Your Darwins, your Mills, your Humes, have never received the endorsement of your prelates. Why, then, criticise my religion on this account?"

"I would not give a fig for a faith that does not tend to elevate mankind's lot on earth as well as his spiritual condition," said one of the group, "and therein I am not prepared to admit the correctness of your statements. Christianity has founded colleges, hospitals and raised the degenerate. It has elevated the downcast and helped its followers to live."

"You are right there to a certain extent," replied the monk calmly, "and yet it is not shown that these things are directly the result of your Christianity. There are many causes operating in the West to produce these results.

"Religious thought should be directed to developing man's spiritual side. Science, art, learning and metaphysical research all have their proper functions in life, but if you seek to blend them, you destroy their individual characteristics until, in time, you eliminate the spiritual, for instance, from the religious altogether. You Americans worship what? The dollar. In the mad rush for gold, you forget the spiritual until you have become a nation of materialists. Even your preachers and churches are tainted with the all-pervading desire. Show me one in the history of your people, who has led the spiritual lives that those whom I can name at home have done. Where are those who, when death comes, could say, 'O Brother Death, I welcome thee.' Your religion helps you to build Ferris wheels and Eiffel towers, but does it aid you in the development of your inner lives?"

The monk spoke earnestly, and his voice, rich and well modulated, came through the dusk that pervaded the apartment, half-sadly, half-accusingly. There was something of the weird in the comments of this stranger from a land whose history dates back 6,000 years upon the civilisation of the Nineteenth Century America.

"But, in pursuing the spiritual, you lost sight of the demands of the present," said some one. "Your doctrine does not help men to live."

"It helps them to die," was the answer.

"We are sure of the present."

"You are sure of nothing."

"The aim of the ideal religion should be to help one to live and to prepare one to die at the same time."

"Exactly," said the Hindu, quickly, "and it is that which we are seeking to attain. I believe that the Hindu faith has developed the spiritual in its devotees at the expense of the material, and I think that in the Western world the contrary is true. By uniting the materialism of the West with the spiritualism of the East I believe much can be accomplished. It may be that in the attempt the Hindu faith will lose much of its individuality."

"Would not the entire social system of India have to be revolutionised to do what you hope to do?"

"Yet, probably, still the religion would remain unimpaired."

The conversation here turned upon the form of worship of the Hindus, and Kananda gave some interesting information on this subject. There are agnostics and atheists in India as well as elsewhere. "Realisation" is the one thing essential in the lives of the followers of Brahma. Faith is not necessary. Theosophy is a subject with which Kananda is not versed, nor is it a part of his creed unless he chooses to make it so. It is more of a separate study. Kananda never met Mme. Blavatsky, but has met Col. Olcott of the American Theosophical Society. He is also acquainted with Annie Besant. Speaking of the "fakirs" of India, the famous jugglers or musicians [magicians?], whose feats have made for them a world-wide reputation, Kananda told of a few episodes that had come within his observation and which almost surpass belief.

"Five months ago," he said, when questioned on this subject, "or just one month before I left India to come to this country, I happened in company in a caravan or party of 25 to sojourn for a space in a city in the interior. While there we learned of the marvellous work of one of these itinerant magicians and had him brought before us. He told us he would produce for us any article we desired. We stripped him, at his request, until he was quite naked and placed him in the corner of the room. I threw my travelling blanket about him and then we called upon him to do as he had promised. He asked what we should like, and I asked for a bunch of California [?] grapes, and straightway the fellow brought them forth from under his blanket. Oranges and other fruits were produced, and finally great dishes of steaming rice."

Continuing, the monk said he believed in the existence of a "sixth sense" and in telepathy. He offered no explanation of the feats of the fakirs, merely saying that they were very wonderful. The subject of idols came up and the monk said that idols formed a part of his religion insomuch as the symbol is concerned.

"What do you worship?" said the monk, "What is your idea of God?"

"The spirit," said a lady quietly.

"What is the spirit? Do you Protestants worship the words of the Bible or something beyond? We worship the God through the idol."

"That is, you attain the subjective through the objective," said a gentleman who had listened attentively to the words of the stranger.

"Yes, that is it," said the monk, gratefully.

Vive Kananda discussed further in the same strain until the call terminated as the hour for the Hindu's lecture approached.

XXXIV

Religious Harmony

(The Detroit Free Press, February 14, 1894)

Swami is a person of medium stature, with the dusky complexion common with people of his nationality, gentle in manner, deliberate in movement, and extremely courteous in every word, movement, and gesture. But the most striking feature of his personality are his eyes, which are of great brilliancy. The conversation naturally drifted upon the subject of religion, when Swami said among many other striking remarks:

"I make the distinction between religion and creed. Religion is the acceptance of all existing creeds, seeing in them the same striving towards the same destination. Creed is something antagonistic and combative. There are different creeds, because there are different people, and the creed is adapted to the commonwealth where it furnishes what people want. As the world is made up of infinite variety of persons of different natures, intellectually, spiritually, and materially, so these people take to themselves that form of belief in the existence of a great and good moral law, which is best fitted for them. Religion recognizes and is glad of the existence of all these forms because of the beautiful underlying principle. The same goal is reached by different routes and my way would not be suited perhaps to the temperament of my Western neighbour, the same that his route would not commend itself to my disposition and philosophical way of thinking. I belong to the Hindu religion. That is not the Buddhists' creed, one of the sects of the Hindu religion. We never indulge in missionary work. We do not seek to thrust the principles of our religion upon anyone. The fundamental principles of our religion forbid that. Nor do we say anything against any missionaries whom you send from this country anywhere. For all of us they are entirely welcome to penetrate the innermost recesses of the earth. Many come to us, but we do not struggle for them; we have no missionaries striving to bring anyone to our way of thinking. With no effort from us many forms of the Hindu religion are spreading far and wide, and these manifestations have taken the form of Christian science, theosophy, and Edwin Arnold's *Light of Asia*. Our religion is older than most religions and the Christian creed — I do not call it religion, because of its antagonistic features — came directly from the Hindu religion. It is one of the great offshoots. The Catholic religion also takes all its forms from us – the confessional, the belief in saints and so on – and a Catholic priest who saw this absolute similarity and recognised the truth of the origin of the Catholic religion was dethroned from his position because he dared to publish a volume explaining all that he observed and was convinced of."

"You recognise agnostics in your religion?" was asked.

"Oh, yes; philosophical agnostics and what you call infidels. When Buddha, who is with us a saint, was asked by one of his followers: 'Does God exist?' He replied: 'God. When have I spoken to you about God? This I tell you, be good and do good.' The philosophical agnostics – there are many of us – believe in the great moral law underlying everything in nature and in the ultimate perfection. All the creeds which are accepted by all people are but the endeavours of humanity to realise that infinity of Self which lies in the great future."

"Is it beneath the dignity of your religion to resort to missionary effort?"

For reply the visitor from the Orient turned to a little volume and referred to an edict among other remarkable edicts.

"This," he said, "was written 200 B.C., and will be the best answer I can give you on that question."

In delightfully clear, well modulated tones, he read:

"The King Piyadasi, beloved of the gods, honours all sects, both ascetics and householders; he propitiates them by alms and other gifts, but he attaches less importance to gifts and honours than to endeavour to promote the essential moral virtues. It is true the prevalence of essential virtues differs in different sects, but there is a common basis. That is, gentleness, moderation in language and morality. Thus one should not exalt one's own sect and decry others, but tender them on every occasion the honour they deserve. Striving thus, one promotes the welfare of his own sect, while serving the others. Striving otherwise, one does not serve his own sect, while disserving others; and whosoever, from attachment to his own sect and with a view to promoting it, decries others, only deals rude blows to his own sect. Hence concord alone is meritorious, so that all bear and love to bear the beliefs of each other. It is with this purpose that this edict has been inscribed; that all people, whatever their fate may be, should be encouraged to promote the essential moral doctrines in each and mutual respects for all other sects. It is with this object that the ministers of religion, the inspectors and other bodies of officers should all work."

After reading this impressive passage Swami Vive Kananda remarked that the same wise king who had caused this edict to be inscribed had forbidden the indulgence of war, as its horrors were antagonistic to all the principles of the great and universal moral doctrine. "For this reason," remarked the visitor, "India has suffered in its material aspect. Where brute strength and bloodshed has advanced other nations, India has deprecated such brutal manifestations; and by the law of the survival of the fittest, which applies to nations as well as to individuals, it has fallen behind as a power on the earth in the material sense."

"But will it not be an impossibility to find in the great combative Western countries, where such tremendous energy is needed to develop the pressing practical necessities of the nineteenth century, this spirit which prevails in placid India?"

The brilliant eyes flashed, and a smile crossed the features of the Eastern brother.

"May not one combine the energy of the lion with the gentleness of the lamb?" he asked.

Continuing, he intimated that perhaps the future holds the conjunction of the East and the West, a combination which would be productive of marvellous results. A condition which speaks well for the natures of the Western nation is the reverence in which women are held and the gentle consideration with which they are treated.

He says with the dying Buddha, "Work out your own salvation. I cannot help you. No man can help you. Help yourself." Harmony and peace, and not dissension, is his watchword.

The following story is one which he related recently regarding the practice of fault-finding among creeds:

"A frog lived in a well. It had lived there for a long time. It was born there and brought up there, and yet was a little, small frog. Of course the evolutionists were not there to tell us whether the frog lost its eyes or not, but, for our story's sake, we must take it for granted that it had eyes, and that it every day cleansed the waters of all the worms and bacilli that lived in it, with an energy that would give credit to our modern bacteriologists. In this way it went on and became a little sleek and fat — perhaps as much so as myself. Well, one day another frog that lived in the sea, came and fell into the well.

"'Whence are you from?'

"'I am from the sea.'

"'The sea? How big is that? Is it as big as my well?' and he took a leap from one side of the well to the other.

"'My friend,' says the frog of the sea, 'how do you compare the sea with your little well?'

"'Then the frog took another leap and asked; 'Is your sea so big?'

"'What nonsense you speak to compare the sea with your well.'

"Well, then,' said the frog of the well, 'nothing can be bigger than my well; there can be nothing bigger than this; this fellow is a liar, so turn him out.'

"That has been the difficulty all the while.

"I am a Hindu. I am sitting in my own little well, and thinking that the world is my well. The Christian sits in his little well and the whole world is his well. The Mohammedan sits in his well and thinks the whole world that. I have to thank you of America for the great attempt you are making to break down the barriers of this little world of ours, and hope that, in the future, the Lord will help you to accomplish that purpose."

XXXV

Fallen Women

(The Detroit Tribune, March 17, 1894)

"Lalun is a member of the most ancient profession in the world. Lilith was her very great-grandmamma, and that was before the days of Eve, as everyone knows. In the West people say rude things about Lalun's profession and write lectures about it, and distribute the lectures to young persons in order that morality may be preserved. In the East, where the profession is hereditary, descending from mother to daughter, nobody writes lectures or takes any notice." – RUDYARD KIPLING.

The story of which the sentences that precede this one are a paragraph, was written in India. They were written by Rudyard Kipling, from whom most of us have learned all that we definitely know about India, with the exception of the fact that India raises wheat enough to be a great competitor of our own farmers, that men work there for two cents a day and that women throw their babies into the Ganga, which is the sacred river of the country.

But Vive Kananda, since he came to this country, has exploded the story about the women of India feeding their babies to the alligators, and now he says that he never heard of Rudyard Kipling until he came to America, and that it is not proper in India to talk of such a profession as that of Lalun, out of which Mr. Kipling has made one of his most delightful and instructive tales.

"In India," said Kananda yesterday, "we do not discuss such things. No one ever speaks of those unfortunate women. When a woman is discovered to be unchaste in India, she is hurled out from her caste. No one thereafter can touch or speak to her. If she went into the house, they would take up and clean the carpets and wash the walls she breathed against. No one can have anything to do with such a person. There are no women who are not virtuous in Indian society. It is not at all as it is in this country. Here there are bad women living side by side with virtuous women in your society. One cannot know who is bad and who is good in America. But in India once a woman slips, she is an outcast for ever – she and her children, sons and daughters. It is terrible, I admit, but it keeps society pure."

"How about the men?" was asked. "Does the same rule hold in regard to them? Are they outcast when they are proven to be unchaste?"

"Oh, no. It is quite different with them. It would be so, perhaps, if they could be found out. But the men move about. They can go from place to place. It is not possible to discover them. The women are shut up in the house. They are certainly discovered if they do anything wrong. And when they are discovered, they are thrown out. Nothing can save them. Sometimes it is very hard when a father has to give up his daughter or a husband his wife. But if they do not give them up, they will be banished with them too. It is very different in this country. Women cannot go about there and make associations as they do here. It is very terrible, but it makes society pure.

"I think that unchastity is the one great sin of your country. It must be so, there is so much luxury here. A poor girl would sell herself for a new bonnet. It must be so where there is so much luxury."

Mr. Kipling says this about Lalun and her profession:

"Lalun's real husband, for even ladies of Lalun's profession have husbands in the East, was a great, big jujube tree. Her mama, who had married a fig, spent ten thousand rupees on Lalun's wedding, which was blessed by forty-seven clergymen of mama's church, and distributed 5,000 rupees in charity to the poor. And that was a custom of the land."

"In India when a woman is unfaithful to her husband she loses her caste, but none of her civil or religious rights. She can still own property and the temples are still open to her.

"Yes," said Kananda, "a bad woman is not allowed to marry. She cannot marry any one without their being an outcast like herself, so she marries a tree, or sometimes a sword. It is the custom. Sometimes these women grow very rich and become very charitable, but they can never regain their caste. In the interior towns, where they still adhere to the old customs, she cannot ride in a carriage, no matter how wealthy she may be; the best that she is allowed is a pair of bullocks. And then in India she has to wear a dress of her own, so that she can be distinguished. You can see these people going by, but no one ever speaks to them. The greatest number of these women is in the cities. A good many of them are Jews too, but they all have different quarters of the cities, you know. They all live apart. It is a singular thing that, bad as they are, wretched as some of these women are, they will not admit a Christian lover. They will not eat with them or touch them — the 'omnivorous barbarians', as they call them. They call them that because they eat everything. Do you know what that disease, the unspeakable disease, is called in India? It is called 'Bad Faringan', which means 'the Christian disease'. It was the Christian that brought it into India.

"Has there been any attempt in India to solve this question? Is it a public question the way it is in America?"

"No, there has been very little done in India. There is a great field for women missionaries if they would convert prostitutes in India. They do nothing in India — very little. There is one sect, the Veshnava [Vaishnava] (Words in square brackets are ours. — Ed.), who try to reclaim these women. This is a religious sect. I think about 90 per cent [?] of all prostitutes belong to this sect. This sect does not believe in caste and they go everywhere without reference to caste. There are certain temples, as the temple of Jagatnot [Jagannath], where there is no caste. Everybody who goes into that town takes off his caste while he is there, because that is holy ground and everything is supposed to be pure there. When he goes outside, he resumes it again, for caste is a mere worldly thing. You know some of the castes are so particular that they will not eat any food unless it is prepared by themselves. They will not touch any one outside their caste. But in the city they all live together. This is the only sect in India that makes proselytes. It makes everybody a member of its church. It goes into the Himalayas and converts the wild men. You perhaps did not know that there were wild men in India. Yes, there are. They dwell at the foot of the Himalayas."

"Is there any ceremony by which a woman is declared unchaste, a civil process?" Kananda was asked.

"No, it is not a civil process. It is just custom. Sometimes there is a formal ceremony and sometimes there is not. They simply make pariahs out of them. When any woman is suspected sometimes they get together and give her a sort of trial, and if it is decided that she is guilty, then a note is sent around to all the other members of the caste, and she is banished.

"Mind you," he exclaimed, "I do not mean to say that this is a solution of the question. The custom is terribly rigid. But you have no solution of the question, either. It is a terrible thing. It is a great wrong of the Western world."